Empire of Sand

Civil War Campaigns and Commanders Series

Battle in the Wilderness: Grant Meets Lee by Grady McWhiney

Death in September: The Antietam Campaign by Perry D. Jamieson

Texans in the Confederate Cavalry by Anne J. Bailey

Sam Bell Maxey and the Confederate Indians by John C. Waugh

The Saltville Massacre by Thomas D. Mays

General James Longstreet in the West: A Monumental Failure by Judith Lee Hallock

The Battle of the Crater by Jeff Kinard

Cottonclads! The Battle of Galveston and the Defense of the Texas Coast by Donald S. Frazier

A Deep Steady Thunder: The Battle of Chickamauga by Steven E. Woodworth

The Texas Overland Expedition of 1863 by Richard Lowe

Raphael Semmes and the Alabama by Spencer C. Tucker

War in the West: Pea Ridge and Prairie Grove by William L. Shea

Iron and Heavy Guns: Duel Between the Monitor and Merrimac by Gene A. Smith

The Emergence of Total War by Daniel E. Sutherland

John Bell Hood and the Struggle for Atlanta by David Coffey

The Most Promising Young Man of the South: James Johnston Pettigrew and His Men at Gettysburg by Clyde N. Wilson

Vicksburg: Fall of the Confederate Gibraltar by Terrence J. Winschel

This Grand Spectacle: The Battle of Chattanooga by Steven E. Woodworth

Rutherford B. Hayes: "One of the Good Colonels" by Ari Hoogenboom

Jefferson Davis's Greatest General: Albert Sidney Johnston by Charles P. Roland

Unconditional Surrender: The Capture of Forts Henry and Donelson by Spencer C. Tucker

Last Stand at Mobile by John C. Waugh

George Gordon Meade and the War in the East by Ethan S. Rafuse

Winfield Scott Hancock: Gettysburg Hero by Perry D. Jamieson

The Last Stronghold: The Campaign for Fort Fisher by Richard B. McCaslin

Sherman's March to the Sea by John F. Marszalek

Campaign for Corinth: Blood in Mississippi by Steven Nathaniel Dossman

Campaign for Wilson's Creek: The Fight for Missouri Begins by Jeffrey L. Patrick

The Red River Campaign: The Union's Final Attempt to Invade Texas by Gary D. Joiner

Empire of Sand

The Struggle for the Southwest, 1862

Thomas W. Cutrer

State House Press

Buffalo Gap, Texas

Library of Congress Cataloging-in-Publication Data

Cutrer, Thomas W.
Empire of Sand: The Struggle for the Southwest, 1862
Thomas W. Cutrer
p. cm.
Includes Bibliographical references and index.
ISBN 978-1-933337-65-4 (pbk. alk. paper)
ISBN- 1-933337-65-6 (pbk. alk. paper)
1. History/United States/Civil War Period (1850-1877) 2. History/United States/State & Local/Southwest(AZ, NM, OK, TX) 3. History/Military/General
This paper meets the requirements of ANSI/NISO, Z39.48-1992 (permanence of paper)
Binding materials have been chosen for durability ∞
I. Title.

"Cataloging-in-Publication Data available from the Library of Congress"

Manufactured in the United States

State House Press
P.O. Box 818
Buffalo Gap, Texas 79508
325-572-3974 · 325-572-3991 (fax)
www.tfhcc.com

Printed in the United States of America
Distributed by Texas A&M University Press Consortium
800-826-8911
www.tamupress.com

ISBN-13: 978-1-933337-65-4
ISBN-10: 1-933337-65-6
Book Design by Rosenbohm Graphic Design

Contents

Biographical Sketches and Maps vii

Preface ix

1 "Terra incognita," New Mexico, 1861 1

2 "Events of the Greatest Consequence":
The Conquest of the Lower Valley 19

3 "1000 Generals": The Army of New Mexico 31

4 "They're Texans. Give Them Hell.":
The Battle of Valverde, February 21, 1862 41

5 "Starvation seems to stare us in the face.":
The Glorieta Campaign, February 22–April 2, 1862 65

6 "It seemed impossible for men to have made their way.":
The Retreat 91

Notes 115

Bibliography 129

Index 133

CAMPAIGNS AND COMMANDERS SERIES

Map Key

Geography

- Trees
- Marsh
- Fields
- Strategic Elevations
- Rivers
- Tactical Elevations
- Fords
- Orchards
- Political Boundaries

Human Construction

- Bridges
- Railroads
- Tactical Towns
- Strategic Towns
- Buildings
- Church
- Roads

Military

- Union Infantry
- Confederate Infantry
- Cavalry
- Artillery
- Headquarters
- Encampments
- Fortifications
- Permanant Works
- Hasty Works
- Obstructions
- Engagements
- Warships
- Gunboats
- Casemate Ironclad
- Monitor
- Tactical Movements
- Strategic Movements

Biographical Sketches

Edward R. S. Canby	7
Henry Hopkins Sibley	10
Ovando J. Hollister	11
James H. Carleton	13
Isaac Lynde	15
John R. Baylor	16
Bethel Coopwood	21
James Reily	33
Tom Green	42
Benjamin S. Roberts	48
Charles Pyron	49
Christopher "Kit" Carson	56
Alexander McRae	57
Samuel A. Lockridge	57
Samuel F. Tappan	74
John P. Slough	75
Gabriel R. Paul	76
John M. Chivington	78
John S. Shropshire	80
William R. Scurry	82
Henry W. Raguet	88
William Steele	104
Sherrod Hunter	107

Maps

New Mexico Territory	xiii
The Valverde Campaign	45
The Battle of Valverde, Phase One	46
The Battle of Valverde, Phase Two	47
The Campaign for New Mexico	66
Glorietta Pass	84

Preface

In June 1861, President Jefferson Davis commissioned Henry Hopkins Sibley, formerly a captain in the Second U.S. Dragoons stationed in New Mexico Territory, as brigadier general in the Confederate Army and authorized him to recruit a brigade of mounted Texans to occupy the mineral-rich Arizona, New Mexico, and Colorado Territories and then to march for the Pacific to seize Los Angeles and San Diego, thus making the infant Confederate republic into a two-ocean empire.

Believing that the citizens of those territories, as well as the U.S. Army regulars stationed there, would not only join his ranks, but also turn over to him their rich stockpiles of military and food resources, on October 22, 1861, Sibley marched west out of El Paso at the head of three regiments—the Fourth, Fifth, and Seventh Texas Mounted Rifles. This 3,200-man brigade, somewhat grandiosely named the Army of New Mexico, reached Fort Bliss by the end of December where it joined Colonel John R. Baylor's battalion of the Second Texas Mounted Rifles, which had, during the previous summer, captured Fort Fillmore and established a Confederate territorial government at Mesilla.

In February 1862, Sibley dispatched Captain Sherrod Hunter and a company of Arizona Rangers to Tucson to recruit volunteers and scout down the Gila River for any movement of Union forces at Fort Yuma. On April 15, Hunter's company skirmished at Picacho Peak with elements of Colonel James Henry Carleton's 1,400-man California Column, which had crossed the Arizona deserts to defend New Mexico and threaten Texas from the west. This was the western-most engagement of the Civil War.

In the meantime, Colonel Edward R. S. Canby, the commander of the Military Department of New Mexico, had been building a 3,800-man force at Fort Craig, seventy miles up the Rio Grande from Mesilla, to resist Sibley's incursion. There he concentrated Federal garrisons from across the territories comprised of the Fifth and Seventh U.S. Infantries and detachments of the First, Second, and Third U.S. Cavalries. He also organized two regiments of New Mexico territorial militia, the First under

Colonel Christopher "Kit" Carson and the Second under Colonel Miguel Estanislado Pino, and received a company of Colorado volunteers.

Not until February 16 did Sibley, having wasted precious weeks, reach Fort Craig, which he now found too strong to assault. Following the advice of two of his regimental commanders, Colonel Tom Green and Lieutenant Colonel William R. Scurry, Sibley crossed the river above the post, thus threatening Canby's line of communication to the north and forcing him to offer battle in the open. Canby resisted the Confederate crossing of the Rio Grande, and on February 21 the two forces clashed at the ford at Valverde. A dramatic Confederate assault crushed the Federal left wing, overrunning and capturing a battery of artillery, but although Canby was forced back into Fort Craig, Sibley did not follow up his victory and found his own supply line to Mesilla interdicted. Although short of food and ammunition, the Texans marched toward Albuquerque, hoping to find supplies there and at Fort Union, the principal military depot in the Southwest. But when the Army of New Mexico, after further critical delays, at last reached Albuquerque on March 2, it found the supplies either removed or destroyed. Although they occupied Santa Fe and Fort Marcy, foul weather further retarded the Rebel advance on Fort Union, one hundred miles up the Santa Fe Trail to the northeast.

On the morning of March 26 the Confederate vanguard—some 400 men commanded by Major Charles L. Pyron—clashed at Apache Canyon with a Federal force comprised of 420 men of the First Colorado Volunteers and U.S. Army regulars from Fort Union, led by Major John M. Chivington. Both sides were soon reinforced, the Federals by the main Union force under Colonel John P. Slough and the Confederates by Colonel Scurry and the remainder of his regiment. The two forces met again at Pigeon's Ranch, near Glorieta Pass, on March 28 with Scurry winning a marginal tactical victory. Slough, however, had detached Chivington and 500 men to march around the Confederate flank and fall on its unguarded supply train. The destruction of the wagons deprived the Rebels of all of their already meager reserve of food and ammunition, forcing them to begin the long, painful withdrawal down the Rio Grande toward El Paso.

With this dramatic reversal of fortune, Canby marched out of Fort Craig with 1,200 men and, on April 8, attacked the small Confederate force occupying Albuquerque, causing Sibley to abandon both that city and Santa Fe. Canby then united with Slough's command and began a lackadaisical pursuit of the exhausted Texans down the Valley. A minor rearguard action was fought at Peralta, some twenty miles south of Albuquerque, on April 15, but otherwise Canby seemed content to let the once powerful Army of New Mexico escape with no further harm.

With Carson's First New Mexico still garrisoning Fort Craig, Sibley was forced to detour to the west around it, through the steep and nearly waterless San Mateo Mountains. By the end of this epic march, Sibley had virtually abdicated command in favor of Green who at last reached Mesilla with only 1,800 men of the original 3,200. The survivors spent May and much of June at Fort Bliss, recovering from their ordeal and gathering supplies for the return journey to San Antonio.

At the end of the campaign, Sibley issued a proclamation to the soldiers of the Army of New Mexico, expressing his "unfeigned pride and pleasure" in congratulating them on the "successes which have crowned their arms in the many encounters with the enemy during the short but brilliant campaign which has just terminated," and assuring them that their performances at Valverde, Glorieta, Albuquerque, and Peralta would be "duly chronicled, and form one of the brightest pages in the history of the Second American Revolution." Private James Franklin Starr of the Fourth Texas Mounted Rifles, for one, was less than sure. Despite Sibley's assurances to the contrary, he believed, "our operations out here will all be lost in history," with New Orleans having fallen and the battle of Shiloh having been fought at the very time that the brigade was fighting at Albuquerque and Peralta and suffering the horrors of its retreat across the mountains around Fort Craig.

And, indeed, until quite recently, the trans-Mississippi West was, to Civil War historiography, what one historian has called "the dark corner of the Confederacy." In particular, the war in the far West remained virtually unchronicled. In the past few decades, however, admirable pioneering work has been done by a number of scholars in editing vital primary documents and producing fine scholarly monographs on the subject. These historians of the trans-Mississippi include Donald S. Frazier, Martin Hardwick Hall, Robert Lee Kerby, Don E. Alberts, Jerry D. Thompson, David B. Gracy, L. Boyd Finch, John Taylor, and Thomas S. Edrington, and only a slight perusal of the footnotes in this volume will quickly reveal the debt that I owe to them. I am pleased to have been able to build on their excellent work, and along with them shed light on the once dark chapter of America's great civil conflict.

I owe also a debt to the McWhiney History Education Group and specifically Donald S. Frazier, CEO and President, and Scott Clowdus, Chief Operations Officer, for undertaking the publishing of this work.

"OUR OPERATIONS OUT HERE WILL ALL BE LOST IN HISTORY"

—Pvt. James Franklin Starr,
Fourth Texas Mounted Rifles

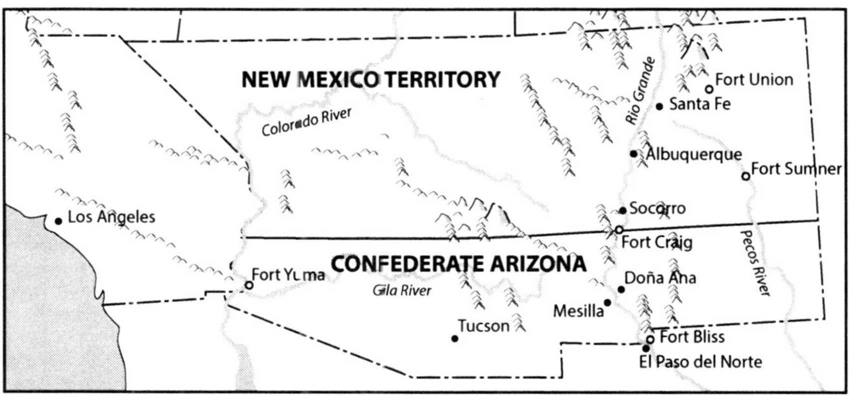

1
"Terra incognita," New Mexico, 1861

The territory seized from Mexico in its disastrous war with the United States "was not exactly terra incognita," reported Colonel George Archibald McCall of the Third U.S. Infantry, "but official Washington . . . knew remarkably little about it. The population, in its size, composition, customs, and attitudes, was largely a matter of conjecture." Even the geography of what became the Territory of New Mexico in September 1850 was imperfectly understood. The valley of the Rio Grande from El Paso north to Santa Fe was reasonably well known, but Governor William Carr Lane told the legislative assembly in December 1852 that the territory was "very distant from the states—difficult of access—and surrounded by barbarians, of doubtful faith. The face of the country is mountainous, and a great elevation—with an appearance of sterility, from a scarcity of water." The population, he reminded them, "does not exceed 60,000 souls" but was so widely scattered that two regiments of U.S. troops were insufficient for its protection. The people of New Mexico were so badly armed that they could not protect themselves, and the economy, based on agriculture and stock-raising, was badly depressed by the lack of a market as well as the lack of protection. The mines, he said, were "nearly abandoned" because their ores did not repay the cost of transportation to markets, and "the schoolmaster, (an indispensable functionary, in a popular government,) is rarely seen amongst you."[1]

The Treaty of Velasco, signed by General Antonio López de Santa Anna in May 1836, ended the war for Texas Independence and established the supposed claim of the Republic of Texas to the Rio Grande as its international boundary. The First Congress of the Republic codified this claim in December 1836, declaring the river, from its source in the present-day state of Colorado to its mouth at Brazos Santiago, to be the western and southern boundary of Texas. The abortive Texan Santa Fe expedition of 1841 failed to validate the Republic's disputed boundary, but when Texas was annexed in 1846, the new state continued to claim eastern New Mexico, including the vital city of Santa Fe. On this assertion, President James K. Polk equivocated. "In regard to the right of Texas to the boundary of the del Norte, from the mouth to the Paso, there cannot," he reported to Congress, "be any serious doubt." Texas's claim to the river as it western boundary, however, Polk questioned. Santa Fe, he observed, had been settled by the Spaniards more than two hundred years previously and had ever since been in the possession of Spain or the Republic of Mexico. "The Texans never have conquered or taken possession if it," he wrote, and the citizens of New Mexico had never been represented in Texas's legislature.[2]

On August 18, 1846, U.S. troops occupied Santa Fe, and the Treaty of Guadalupe Hidalgo, which ended the Mexican War, established the Rio Grande as far west as El Paso as the international boundary. Texas's claim to eastern New Mexico, however, remained in dispute. When a civil government for New Mexico Territory was established, therefore, Texas governor J. Pinckney Henderson protested that the central government was usurping his state's sovereignty.[3]

By 1848, however, the House of Representatives was increasingly unwilling to sponsor the expansion of slavery into western territories and therefore determined to abrogate Texas's claim. The Texas Legislature countered by moving to organize Santa Fe County, with boundaries encompassing the largest part of New Mexico east of the Rio Grande, and by passing a joint resolution informing the U.S. Congress that the territory was an integral part of Texas.

Because most of the citizens of northern New Mexico were both of Hispanic descent and of antislavery inclination, and because of a long history of enmity toward Texas, the region displayed a determined disinclination to sanction the authority of the new county. In October 1848, a mass meeting in Santa Fe protested incorporation into the Lone Star State, and on May 25, 1850, delegates signed a free-soil constitution for New Mexico Territory, specifying boundaries that included the putative Santa Fe County.

Texans demanded that rebellious New Mexico be subdued by military force, and the more radical Texans even called for immediate secession if the federal government chose to interfere with its claim to a Rio Grande boundary. On August 13, 1850, Governor Peter H. Bell informed a special session of the Texas Legislature of his "deliberate and firm conviction that there is now left us but one course consistent with honor, and a just sense of what is due to ourselves as a sovereign community." That course was the adoption "of such measures as are necessary for the occupation of Santa Fe, with a force ample to quell the arrogant and rebellious spirit now prevailing there, and to enable us to extend and firmly establish the jurisdiction and laws of the State over it."

Given New Mexico's reluctance to become a part of Texas, and the U.S. government's apparent support of that territory's wishes, Governor Bell recommended that the legislature authorize him to raise "at least two regiments of mounted volunteers for the contemplated move to and occupancy of Santa Fe." Political leaders from the lower South, fearing that a free-soil New Mexico would effectively block the expansion of the region's "peculiar institution," thereby dooming it to extinction, responded by sending Bell offers of moral and even military support.[4]

However eager Texas might have been to occupy New Mexico by force, a military occupation of the disputed territory would be challenged by the U.S. Army, "a lion in her path," in the words of New Jersey senator

William Lewis Dayton. A defiant Texas threatened military confrontation, and Senator Sam Houston claimed that three thousand volunteers had already been ordered to occupy eastern New Mexico. President Millard Fillmore and General-in-Chief and Secretary of War, ad interim, Winfield Scott issued orders to the commander of the Ninth Military District, Brevet Colonel John Munroe, to resist Texas aggression with all means at his command, whereupon Texas at last yielded the point.[5]

Despite the region's apparent poverty of resources and population and Texas's repeated failures to occupy the territory, to the Jefferson Davis administration in Richmond, Virginia, the Southwest seemed a golden apple, ripe for the picking. To Lieutenant Colonel John R. Baylor, who was to command the first forces to enter the territory under the Confederate flag, the region's "vast mineral resources" were a great prize for the South to win. "In addition," he wrote, "its affording an outlook to the Pacific, makes its acquisition a matter of some importance to our government."[6]

A large portion of the U.S. Army—some one thousand regulars—was garrisoning forts in the territory at the outbreak of the war, and the Confederacy saw them as a source of arms and ammunition. In the early summer of 1861, M. H. McWilley, a resident of Mesilla, wrote to Davis that "the stores, supplies, and munitions of war within New Mexico and Arizona are immense, and I am decidedly of the opinion that the game is well worth the ammunition." Even more pointedly, William Lott Davidson, who served as a private in the Fifth Texas Mounted Rifles during the New Mexico campaign but ultimately became the regiment's lieutenant colonel, made the claim that "many thousand stands of arms belonging to the United States government" were stored in the forts of Arizona and New Mexico and that many of the citizens, as well as many officers of the U.S. Army then stationed in the region, "would love to fly our standard and enlist under our banner."[7]

There, as elsewhere in the old army, a great many professional officers were of Southern sentiment. The surgeon at Fort Fillmore "found the garrison and people in the neighboring towns of Mesilla, Las Cruces, and Doña Anna in great excitement and agitation at the near approach of hostilities between the north and south," and an unnamed U.S. soldier at Fort Marcy near Santa Fe observed that "nothing is talked of here but secession. All the officers seemed for it.[8]

William Need, a New Mexico Unionist, stated the popular opinion that Davis's "military prototypes and protégés" were only waiting for the secession of their home states to lead their units out of the U.S. Army and to turn over the territory to the Confederacy. These officers included Colonel William H. Loring, the commander of the Department of New Mexico, as well as two future corps commanders of the Army of Northern Virginia, James Longstreet and Richard S. Ewell, and such lesser lights as Colonel Thomas Turner Fauntleroy of the First Dragoons, Lieutenant Colonel George Bibb Crittenden of the Regiment of Mounted Rifles, Lieutenant Colonel John Breckenridge Grayson of the Second Artillery, Major Alexander Welch Reynolds of the First Infantry, Major Thomas Grimke Rhett of the Mounted Rifles, Major Henry Hopkins Sibley of the First Dragoons, and First Lieutenant Alexander Early Steen of the Third Infantry. In total, ten field grade officers, all of whom had been stationed in New Mexico by Davis himself, as Franklin Pierce's secretary of war, or by James Buchannan's pro-secession secretary of war, John B. Floyd, purportedly "to second and forward his ulterior designs" of seizing the territory for the South, resigned to accept Confederate commissions. Indeed, prominent newspaper editor Horace Greeley went so far as to claim that Loring and Crittenden planned to turn their commands in New Mexico "over to the service and support of the Rebellion" by marching them into Texas, only to be foiled when Lieutenant Colonel Benjamin S. Roberts revealed their plan.[9]

But for more than any other reason, the southwest territories presented a potential empire for slavery. As Trevanian T. Teel, a prominent Texas attorney and ardent secessionist expressed it, with New Mexico, Arizona, California, and Utah in Southern hands, "there would be plenty of room for the extension of slavery, which would greatly strengthen the Confederate States."[10]

A large portion of the white population of New Mexico, especially those of the lower Rio Grande valley, favored secession. Most had migrated from the Southern states, and although the practice of slavery was scarcely profitable there, the territory seemed ready to cast its lot with the Confederacy. Even before Abraham Lincoln's inauguration, the Santa Fe *Gazette* offered the opinion that "to attempt to subjugate the southern states looks very much like an absurd project. The southern people will fight until the last drop of blood shall have been shed, or until the invader shall have been driven from the soil."[11]

On March 16, 1861, a meeting at Mesilla, calling itself a "convention of the people of Arizona," repudiated the U.S. government and "attached themselves to the Confederate states" for territorial organization and protection. The members of the assembly resolved that "we will not recognize the present black Republican administration, and that we will resist any officers appointed to this territory by said administration with whatever means in our power." Five months later, a convention held at Tucson declared Arizona a Confederate territory and elected Virginia-born Granville H. Oury, a district judge and prominent mine owner, as a delegate to the Confederate Congress.[12]

Thus, the threat of a Southern annexation of the Southwest was not only clear and present but immense. As Captain Gurden Chapin, the acting inspector general at Santa Fe wrote to Henry W. Halleck, the conquest of the region "is a great political feature of the rebellion. It will give the rebels a name and prestige [in] Europe, and operate against the Union cause. It therefore should not only be checked, but it should . . . be rendered impossible."[13]

But as Private William Henry "Hank" Smith of the Fifth Texas Mounted Rifles was to observe, although secessionist sentiment on the lower Rio Grande bore out the South's expectation of an easy conquest, farther upstream "the territory's population became increasingly Hispanic and less old stock Anglo-southern. The people of northern New Mexico had been invaded by Texans before, and distrusted them whatever flag they now carried."[14]

Edward R. S. Canby

Canby was born Kentucky in 1817 and graduated thirtieth of thirty-one cadets in the U.S. Military Academy class of 1839. Commissioned as a second lieutenant in the Second U.S. Infantry, he was promoted to first lieutenant on the eve of the outbreak of the war with Mexico in 1846. Canby served in Major General Winfield Scott's army in the Mexico City campaign, taking part in the siege of Veracruz and the battles of Cerro Gordo, Contreras, and Churubusco, and the capture of Mexico City. He received brevet promotions through the rank of lieutenant colonel for "gallant and meritorious conduct."

Following the war, he was assigned to staff duty in California where he was transferred to the Tenth U.S. Infantry, and in 1855, he was promoted to the substantive grade of major. At the outbreak of the Civil War, he was the colonel of the Nineteenth U.S. Infantry and commander of the Department of New Mexico with headquarters at Fort Defiance. One of his officers described him as "portly and commanding, his manner dignified and self-possessed, his whole appearance such as to inspire confidence and respect from his fellows." He had "an air of superiority, largely the gift of nature, though undoubtedly strengthened by long habits of command." Another of the Colorado volunteers, Alonzo Ferdinand Ickis, wrote that Canby "is a fine looking man all of six feet and straight, perhaps fifty years of age. He has the appearance of great firmness but does not does not put on as many airs as most of the captains."

After commanding the Federal forces that repulsed Confederate brigadier general Henry Hopkins Sibley's invasion of New Mexico, Canby was made a brigadier general of U.S. Volunteers for his role in the battle of Valverde and assigned to duty as commander of the Military Division of West Mississippi. He commanded the army that captured Mobile, Alabama, on April 12, 1865, for which he was promoted to major general of U.S. Volunteers, and at the war's end received the surrender of the last two Confederate armies in the field, those of Lieutenant General Richard Taylor and Lieutenant. General Edmund Kirby Smith. Promoted to brigadier general of the U.S. Army in 1866, he was assigned to the command of the Department of Columbia and then the Division of the Pacific. Canby was assassinated on April 11, 1873, in Siskiyou County, California, by a band of Modoc Indians led by their chief, Captain Jack, during negotiations for their removal to a reservation.

On May 17, 1861, the War Department directed Colonel Loring to forward the Fifth and Seventh Infantry regiments and two companies of the Tenth Infantry, under the command of brevet Lieutenant Colonel Edward R. S. Canby, to Fort Leavenworth, Kansas, "with as little delay as practicable." Upon learning of Loring's resignation, however, the War Department rescinded Canby's orders, promoting him to colonel and ordering him from Fort Defiance to Santa Fe as military commander of the territory. To replace the troops that were still to march east, he was authorized to raise two regiments of New Mexico volunteers.[15]

One of Canby's officers described him as "portly and commanding, his manner dignified and self-possessed, his whole appearance such as to inspire confidence and respect from his fellows." He had "an air of superiority, largely the gift of nature, though undoubtedly strengthened by long habits of command." His habitual civilian costume contrasted with the "boiled rags of the military fops" around him. But whether Canby was "the man for the posish," Colorado volunteer Alonzo Ferdinand Ickis hesitated to predict, "time will tell." Although many of his officers eventually came to a different conclusion, Ovando J. Hollister, the captain of the cavalry company of the First Colorado Volunteers, saw in the colonel "a man of foresight and judgment—patient, prudent and cautious—of great courage, both moral and physical, and as true to the government as any man in existence."[16]

The new district commander found the people of the territory to be "apathetic in disposition," and willing to "adopt any measure that may be necessary for the defense of their territory with great tardiness, looking with great concern to their private and often petty interests and delaying or defeating the objects of the government by their personal or political quarrels." In particular, Canby informed the War Department, "the Mexican people have no affection for the institutions of the United States; they have a strong, but hitherto restrained, hatred for the Americans as a race." Moreover, according to the district commander, individuals in the Hispanic community were "secretly but industriously" endeavoring "to keep alive the all the elements of discontent and fan them into flames."[17]

Canby had no faith in the loyalty or military potential of the New Mexicans, to whom he referred as "these ignorant and impulsive people." In the organization of native volunteers, he advised Major Isaac Lynde, then commanding strategically vital Fort Fillmore, "I have endeavored to secure at least one American who could be relied upon among the commissioned officers of each company. It is desirable that the same principle should be observed in organizing the companies that you may call for in your neighborhood."[18]

Navajos and Apaches in Arizona and New Mexico interdicted mail service to California, burned supply trains, appropriated livestock, and killed more than two hundred whites during the four years of the Civil War, thus creating the necessity of retaining Union troops in the Southwest, who would otherwise have been deployed in other theaters of the war. Thus, Canby had fewer troops of a less reliable quality to fight not only the Navajos and Apaches, against whom he had just passed "a very trying winter campaign of six months' duration," but also whatever Confederate force might be launched against his department. Soon after assuming command, Canby was confronted with the intelligence that two expeditions were forming against him—one out of Texas under Major General Earl Van Dorn, to attack Fort Union by way of the Canadian River; the other under Brigadier General Sibley at San Antonio, to reinforce Lieutenant Colonel Baylor's battalion at El Paso for a drive up the Rio Grande. He was, therefore, compelled to keep a strong force at Fort Union and another at Fort Craig, and to hold a third in reserve to support either point that might come under attack. Canby believed that volunteers could be used against Indians, but should be used only as auxiliaries against the Confederates. To fill his ranks with dependable soldiers, Canby informed Governor William Gilpin of Colorado Territory that "it might be necessary to ask your excellency to organize four or six companies in the Colorado Territory."[19]

Colorado, however, was not without a secessionist movement of its own. In July 1861, "the disaffected in Denver boldly announced their principles, raised a Secesh flag," and according to Hollister, "secretly

Henry Hopkins Sibley

Sibley was born in Natchitoches, Louisiana, on May 25, 1816. He graduated from West Point in 1838 and was commissioned a second lieutenant in the Second U.S. Dragoons. After seeing action in the Second Seminole War, Sibley was promoted to captain and given command of Company I of the Second Dragoons, and serving in Winfield Scott's army in Mexico, he took part in the battles of Veracruz, Cerro Gordo, Contreras, Churubusco, and Molino del Rey, for which he received a brevet promotion to major. From 1850 to 1854 Sibley and his company were stationed at various forts on the Texas frontier before receiving a transfer to Kansas to quell the violence between pro-slavery elements and Free-Soilers there. In 1857 the regiment took part in the so-called Mormon War. In Utah, Sibley was court-martialed as a result of a feud with his regimental commander, Philip St. George Cooke. Transferred to New Mexico Territory, the Second Dragoons took part in the unsuccessful Navajo Campaign of 1860, and there, Sibley resigned from the army to go to Richmond, Virginia, where he persuaded Jefferson Davis to accept his plan to seize California and the Southwest for the Confederacy. As a brigadier general, Sibley organized what he grandiosely styled "the Army of New Mexico" at San Antonio and launched an invasion of New Mexico. After defeating the Federals in the battle of Valverde on February 21, 1862, his "army"—in fact, no more than a brigade of Texan cavalry—marched up the Rio Grande to capture Albuquerque and Santa Fe before moving on to Fort Union, the last Union stronghold in the territory. Although defeating John P. Slough's command in the field at Glorieta Pass on March 28, 1862, a Federal raiding party under John M. Chivington fell upon the Rebel rear and destroyed their meager supply train, forcing them to begin an arduous retreat toward El Paso. Having not only failed in his mission to conquer the region for the South, but having lost a third of his command in New Mexico, Sibley was summoned to Richmond to answer charges of poor leadership. He resumed command of his brigade again under Major General Richard Taylor in Louisiana in 1863, but total loss of the respect of his command, combined with his heavy drinking, led to his court-martial, and although acquitted, he was replaced in command of the cavalry brigade by Tom Green. After the war Sibley was recruited into the Egyptian army in 1869 to oversee the construction of coastal fortifications, but because of his alcoholism and incompetence, he was dismissed in 1873. He died in Fredericksburg, Virginia, on August 23, 1886.

Ovando J. Hollister

Hollister, the captain of the cavalry company of the First Colorado Volunteers, was born in Coleraine, Massachusetts, on October 7, 1834, but he moved to Colorado Territory in the spring of 1860. Hollister was discharged from his regiment in 1863 as a result of injuries. Thereafter, from November 1863 through December 1865, he became editor and half-owner of the *Daily Mining Journal* in Gilpin County. In 1868, after serving as editor of the *Rocky Mountain News*, he was appointed collector of internal revenue at Salt Lake City, Utah. During that period he became a prolific writer, publishing, in addition to *The History of the First Regiment of Colorado Volunteers, The Mines of Colorado* (1867), *A Complete and Comprehensive Description of the Agricultural, Stock Raising and Mineral Resources of Utah* (1879), and *Polygamy: Or, The Mysteries and Crimes of Mormonism: Being a Full and Authentic History of this Strange Sect from Its Origin to the Present Time, With a Thrilling Account of the Inner Life and Teachings of the Mormons* (1882). He was married to the half-sister of Vice President Schuyler Colfax, whose biography he published in 1886. Hollister died on February 12, 1892, in Salt Lake City, Utah.

bought up all arms, and in various ways commenced marshaling their forces to seize our infant territory." The reported movement of "Baylor's Babe's" up the Rio Grande induced Governor William Gilpin to purchase all of the arms in the country, "not so much for the use of the volunteers as to prevent traitors from getting them." More importantly, Gilpin authorized the formation of a regiment of volunteers. At that time, Hollister, a none-too-successful miner in the South Clear Creek district of the Colorado Rocky Mountains, was discussing with two fellow prospectors a method of earning an easier living. "Casting their eyes about for a new lode," Hollister later wrote, "the state of the country, plunged in a gigantic civil war, attracted their attention, and the idea of taking advantage of the patriotic uprising of the nation's heart and the hard times and the mines, to raise a company of volunteers for the war, the securing commissions for themselves, struck them as being a lode, which, once open, might be worked with ease and profit." They soon printed a recruiting poster for a mounted "mountain company," which promised free transportation back to the United States—"a sentiment sufficiently powerful of itself to enlist a company" during the hard times then visiting the mines—and service under the notorious Kansas Jayhawker, James Henry Lane. By mid-August, more than eighty men had answered the call.[20]

The company organized itself in Denver, "expecting to start for the states, as soon as the requisite transportation could be forwarded." Governor Gilpin, however—aware that a Colorado secession movement had "always been well represented in our society"—was unwilling to have these men leave the territory, where he was recruiting volunteers "to preserve Colorado for the Union." Gilpin, therefore, induced the volunteers—to the dissatisfaction of many who had enlisted with the idea of "going to the states and taking an active part in the war"—to join what became the First Colorado Volunteers, a mixed regiment of infantry and cavalry companies, with John P. Slough commissioned as colonel, Samuel F. Tappan, a prominent abolitionist in the "Bleeding Kansas" controversy, as lieutenant colonel, and John M. Chivington as major. Because of the presence of this regiment, Hollister believed, "Colorado escaped the civil convulsions that have desolated portions of our once happy country."[21]

The Confederate drive into the Southwest caused considerable alarm in California, as well. According to Allen Latham Anderson, a captain in the Fifth U.S. Infantry, later to become the colonel of the Eighth California Infantry, "the remote and unimportant territory of New Mexico" was not the true objective of the Rebel thrust up the Rio Grande. The Confederates, in fact, were "striking at much higher game—no less than the conquest of California, Sonora, Chihuahua, New Mexico, Arizona, and Utah—and, above all, the possession of the gold supply of the Pacific coast."[22]

As many as one-third of the California's citizens were of Southern birth and sympathies, and especially in the southern half of the state, where

James Carleton

Carleton was born in Lubec, Maine, on December 27, 1814, and received a commission as a second lieutenant in the First U.S. Dragoons directly from civilian life in October 1839. After service against Indians on the western frontier, his regiment was assigned to Brigadier General Zachary Taylor's army in Mexico where Carleton saw action at the battle of Buena Vista, for which he received a brevet promotion to the rank of major. Carleton spent most of the following ten years assigned to duty in New Mexico Territory, but in 1859 was ordered to Salt Lake City to investigate the so-called Mountain Meadows Massacre. From Utah, he was transferred to California where he was stationed at the outbreak of the Civil War. On August 19, 1861, he was appointed colonel of the First California Infantry and then in April 1862 was promoted to brigadier general of volunteers and assigned to the command of the "California Column." In September 1862 he superseded Edward R. S. Canby as commander of the Department of New Mexico.

With the threat of Confederate annexation of the New Mexico abated by Brigadier General Henry H. Sibley's withdrawal from the territory, Carleton turned his attention to the pacification of the Mescalero Apache, sending Colonel Christopher "Kit" Carson on an expedition to relocate the tribe to the reservation at Bosque Redondo on the Pecos River. With this mission accomplished by February 1863, Carleton launched Carson's column against the Navajos, resulting in the surrender and internment of some eight thousand Navajos at Bosque Redondo. Carleton's hopes of seeing the tribesmen converted to Christianity and an agrarian lifestyle ended in failure, and although his superiors considered him to be an efficient and capable administrator, territorial politics led to his reassignment as lieutenant colonel of the Fourth U.S. Cavalry, then stationed in Texas, early in 1867. Carleton died in San Antonio on January 7, 1873.

the majority of that population was concentrated, secessionist rhetoric and personal violence were common, and the only Union force standing between Baylor's Texans and Los Angeles was the small garrison at Fort Yuma. Although the majority of Californians were staunch Unionists, and according to philosopher and historian Josiah Royce, "could not have been led out of the Union by the most skillful party of managers," shortly after the bombardment of Fort Sumter, Brigadier General Edwin V. Sumner, the commander of the Department of the Pacific, reinforced the garrisons at San Bernardino and Los Angeles to prevent a Rebel uprising.[23]

Late in July 1861 the War Department sent a requisition to California governor John Gatley Downey for a regiment of infantry and five companies of cavalry to guard the Overland Mail route in Nevada and Utah, specifying that the command be given to Major James H. Carleton of the First Dragoons. These companies were quickly filled with what George Gwyther, the surgeon of the First California Cavalry, characterized as "stalwart, big-bearded men, hardened and bronzed to every vicissitudes of miners' and farmer's life." Although specifically recruited to guard the Overland route, upon learning of the Confederate designs on New Mexico Territory, Sumner diverted Carleton's so-called "California Column" to southern California to guard the Santa Fe Trail from Fort Yuma. Soon after Carleton, by then promoted to colonel, occupied Los Angeles, Brigadier General George Wright replaced Sumner as department commander. The aggressive Wright quickly determined that by marching into New Mexico from the west, the California Column might interdict the Rebel line of communication with Fort Davis, reopen the southern mail route, and avert the Confederate threat to both Colorado and the Pacific.[24]

Troops from Colorado and California would not, however, reach New Mexico for some weeks, and Canby saw that the forces under his command were too thinly spread to hold all of the installations in his district. In response to the War Department directive that he distribute his remaining regulars "at such points as would best protect the interests of the United States government," in mid-June he ordered Major Lynde to abandon Fort McLane and take over the command of Fort Fillmore near Mesilla, "a nice clean post, big and airy quarters," about half-mile from the left bank of the Rio Grande, forty miles above El Paso, a strategic point on the threatened Confederate invasion route into New Mexico. At the same time, he ordered that several other forts in the territory be abandoned.[25]

Isaac Lynde

Lynde was a native of Vermont and a graduated from West Point in the class of 1827, finishing thirty-second in a class of thirty-eight. Assigned first to the Fifth U.S. Infantry after undistinguished service in the war with Mexico, he was promoted to major and reassigned to the Seventh U.S. Infantry on October 15, 1859. His regimental surgeon, James Cooper McKee, considered him to be "quiet, restrained, and retired, giving the impression of wisdom and the knowledge of his profession." In the early days of his command at Fort Fillmore, therefore, McKee "looked up to him with more than ordinary admiration and confidence, thinking and reasoning with myself that, being old and long experienced, with not many years to live, certainly he did not fear death, and could be depended on to defend the honor of the flag." As might have been expected, with the surrender of his regiment Lynde was summarily dismissed from service by order of President Abraham Lincoln, in November 1861. On November 27, 1866, however, President Andrew Johnson revoked the order and restored him to duty to date from July 28, 1866, and on the same date placed him on the retired list.

On August 2, 1861, Colonel Roberts, destroyed the public stores at Fort Stanton and marched for Fort Craig. The Federals also evacuated all of present-day Arizona, with the garrisons of Fort Buchanan, near Tubac, and Fort Breckinridge, near the confluence of the San Pedro and the Gila rivers, ordered to report to Major Lynde at Fort Fillmore. Lynde, a West Point graduate and veteran of thirty-four years of service, reached Fillmore in the first week of July. Post surgeon James Cooper McKee, who was to become his most vocal critic, observed that his gray hair and gray beard gave him "a venerable appearance." In time, however, as he perceived that "no effort was made to put the command and fighting trim, no measures taken to ensure us against surprises," the surgeon came to doubt the commander's courage and efficiency.[26]

The immediate threat to the southern flank of the New Mexico Territory came from a battalion of Texas cavalry commanded by Lieutenant Colonel Baylor. Baylor, a Kentucky native, as a small boy

John R. Baylor

Baylor was born in Paris, Kentucky, on July 27, 1822, but moved with his family as a boy to Fort Gibson, Indian Territory, where his father was the assistant surgeon of the Seventh U.S. Infantry. Upon the death of his father he took up residence with his uncle in Fayette County, Texas. In 1842 he returned to Fort Gibson to teach school at the Creek agency. One year later he was with his brother-in-law, James Dawson, when Dawson killed an Indian trader named Seaborn Hill. Charged as an accomplice, Baylor fled to Fayette County, Texas, where he became a farmer and rancher. In 1851 he was elected to the state legislature, and two years later he was admitted to the bar. In September 1855 he was appointed agent to the Comanches on the Clear Fork of the Brazos but was dismissed in 1857 as a result of a disagreement with his supervisor over the culpability of the reservation Indians for raids on the frontier. For several years thereafter, he led a crusade against the Indians, addressing mass meetings, organizing a vigilante force of some one thousand men, which he led against the Comanche at the battle of Paint Creek in June 1860, and editing an anti-Indian newspaper, the *White Man.*

When Texas seceded from the Union, Baylor was commissioned as the lieutenant colonel of the Second Texas Mounted Rifles and ordered to occupy a chain of forts protecting the overland route between San Antonio and El Paso. Baylor reached Fort Bliss in July 1861, occupied the Mesilla Valley, and without a fight, captured Fort Fillmore and the Seventh U.S. Infantry under Major Isaac Lynde at San Augustine Pass on July 27, 1861. He thereupon established the Confederate Territory of Arizona at Mesilla and proclaimed himself military governor. He was promoted to colonel in December, but as a result of a fatal duel with the editor of the Mesilla *Times* and his brutal treatment of the region's Apache population, President Jefferson Davis removed him from command. Baylor returned to Texas where he fought as a private soldier in the battle of Galveston, January 1, 1863, and won election to the Second Confederate Congress. In April 1865 he regained his former military rank but saw no further action.

After the war he moved to San Antonio, and in 1873 he was unsuccessful in his bid for the Democratic nomination for governor. In 1878 he acquired a sizable ranch near Montell on the Nueces River. There he reputedly killed a fellow rancher but was never charged with the crime. He died at Montell on February 6, 1894.

had moved with his family to Fort Gibson, Indian Territory, where his father was an assistant surgeon in the Seventh Infantry. Baylor had a series of run-ins with Indians, Mexicans, and others, until his arrival in Texas and election to the state legislature. From then until the time that Texas seceded, he carried on a personal vendetta against the Indians, addressing mass meetings, editing an anti-Indian newspaper, the *White Man*, and organizing a vigilante force of some one thousand men that he led in June 1860 against a band of Comanches accused of the murder of a white boy.[27]

Despite his reputation for extreme violence and a seething hatred for American Indians, Baylor was apparently highly energetic and charismatic, and at least one of his soldiers considered him "a complete gentleman," and in May 1861, Baylor, was commissioned as lieutenant colonel of John S. Ford's Second Texas Mounted Rifles. Following the regiment's service in securing the Federal forts on the Rio Grande and in the Nueces Strip in the spring of 1861, it received orders to occupy the chain of evacuated Federal posts protecting the overland route between Fort Clark and Fort Bliss and then to push up the Rio Grande to establish a Confederate Territory of Arizona, to be carved from the southern half of New Mexico Territory. Ford remained in Austin as head of the recruiting bureau, but Baylor, then commanding the regiment, was to become the governor of the new Confederate territory . . . "when we take it," one of his soldiers wrote.[28]

2
"Events of the Greatest Consequence": The Conquest of the Lower Valley

On April 1, 1861, the first company of volunteers left San Antonio to occupy Fort Davis. One of the company considered the march to be an "extended hunting and fishing and drinking expedition," subsisting largely on fish and turkeys caught or killed en route, but by the end of June the company was "thoroughly sick of garrison duty." When, therefore, on July 1, Sergeant Morgan Wolfe Merrick, recorded in his diary, "we see from the papers that there is some prospect of troops being sent to New Mexico and Arizona," the bored volunteers were jubilant. One week later, the company was, as Merrick wrote "on the road again." As Milam Taylor, a private in Lieutenant Colonel John R. Baylor's battalion, reported to his father, "We heard the abolitionists were going to take Fort Bliss, and we started on a forced march, traveling day and night.[1]

Supplied with two wagons, the company made good time between watering places, and, at first at least, Merrick recorded that the country "looks nice, reminds one of meadows and orchard" with an occasional herd of antelope or prairie dog town to break the monotony of the march. "If this country had streams of water running through it, it sure would be a charming place to live." Past Van Horn, however, the route became "a godforsaken looking country," and Merrick complained that "the farther we go the rougher it gets." The road was sandy and vegetation was sparse. "We have been looking for a change in the topography, but now it's the same old thing." Approaching El Paso "the better condition of the country" became evident. Herds of sheep and of cattle began to appear, and "things in general began to show that people are living not far off." Baylor "was warmly welcomed by the few secessionists in that neighborhood," and the battalion, some three hundred strong, at last arrived at Fort Bliss on July 15. "This is a beautiful post," Merrick wrote, with "fine large shade trees in front of our quarters."[2]

Baylor immediately began preparations to occupy the Mesilla Valley, and after a week's rest at Fort Bliss, Merrick reported "quite a buzz around the quarters." The battalion received orders on July 22 to march up the Rio Grande, and "tonight," he predicted, "we will camp no doubt in the enemy's territory, that is New Mexico." Baylor's scouts reported that the Federals "were concentrating in strong force at Fort Fillmore, and from the proximity of the post I supposed that the object of the enemy was to attack the forces under my command at Fort Bliss." Fearing that if they were allowed to concentrate, his battalion would be too weak to effectively resist, he determined to attack the enemy in detail. After a reconnaissance patrol assured him that Fillmore was vulnerable not only to a surprise attack but also to the interdiction of its water supply, Baylor and 258 men marched out of Fort Bliss on the night of July 23, and by the following night had reached Mesilla. That night, Captain Bethel Coopwood's independent company, the "San Elisario Spies and Guides," made a raid on the livestock herd, which put most of the Federal cavalry afoot and made the Confederacy "richer by two hundred head of horses and mules."[3]

Nevertheless, the Texans were convinced that in storming the fort they would have "a hard, and perhaps bloody fight; so says all that pretend to

Bethel Coopwood

Coopwood was born on May 1, 1827, in Lawrence County, Alabama. He moved to Tyler County, Texas, in 1846 and became an able lawyer and scholar of Spanish colonial history in the lower Rio Grande Valley. He served as a private in Colonel Peter Hansboro Bell's regiment of Texas Mounted Volunteers in the war with Mexico, but in 1854 he moved to Los Angeles, California, where he was admitted to the bar. With the state's secession, Coopwood returned to Texas and in El Paso was elected as captain of the San Elizario Spy Company. Stricken by illness, he was absent during much of the New Mexico campaign and left the army in 1863. After the Civil War, Coopwood spent a year in Coahuila but returned to the practice of law in Texas where he served as a judge. He died in Austin on December 26, 1907. A. B. Peticolas characterized him as "a brave man, a good fighter, and deserves promotion for successfully guiding the brigade through the mountains around Craig."

know." Baylor estimated the garrison at Fillmore to number between six and seven hundred regulars, whereas his own command numbered less than three hundred. Nevertheless, as Taylor wrote, the Texans were "all getting very tired of being confined" in Fort Bliss, "and long to go into action; although some of us may never come out of it alive."[4]

Although Major Isaac Lynde was well aware that the Rebels were nearby, Surgeon James Cooper McKee noted that "not a picket [was posted] for our security or to prevent a surprise." On the night of July 24, the Rebels approached within six hundred yards of Fillmore, and according to Taylor, "were waiting until next morning at daybreak to storm the fort by surprise." Baylor's men believed that the assault "would have been a complete success, but one of our pickets deserted and went up to the fort and gave the alarm, and in a few minutes the fort was alive." McKee agreed that had not one of the Confederate pickets alarmed the garrison "their success would have been complete." Instead, "drums beat the long roll, the command turned out, and we were saved for the time." But Lynde "took no further active steps, not sending out any scout to see where the enemy were. All was left to Providence."[5]

Balked of his chance to take Fillmore by coup de main, Baylor retired to Mesilla on the afternoon of July 25. The village, Baylor believed, "could be easily held," and in Confederate hands, "would enable them to hold the country." According to the Mesilla *Times*, Baylor's Texans were received with every manifestation of joy. "Forage and supplies were freely offered by the overjoyed citizens, who declared they were weary of Yankee tyranny and oppression." With a population of a little more than two thousand—"all Mexican except several merchants and gamblers," claimed Sergeant Merrick—Mesilla was the second-largest settlement in the New Mexico Territory and the largest in what became Confederate Arizona. Little more, in fact than the rawest kind of frontier village, Mesilla boasted a weekly newspaper, several large mercantile firms, and a host of saloons and gambling dens.[6]

Threatened by the Rebel occupation of Mesilla, Lynde moved to drive them out. Leaving one company of infantry and the Seventh Infantry band at Fort Fillmore, Lynde crossed the Rio Grande on July 25 with a force of infantry, cavalry, and a two-gun battery, numbering, according to various accounts, between 380 and 500 men, all "well-disciplined and reliable soldiers." Baylor's Texans and "the 'Yanks'" had been "exchanging compliments and threatening to hurt each other for the past eight months," wrote William Davidson, and at Mesilla "they tried each other on."[7]

Informed that the Federals were marching to the attack, Baylor posted his men on the tops of the adobe houses and in a corral south of town and awaited their arrival, late in the afternoon. "They formed within 300 yards, and were, as near as I can tell, about 600 strong," Baylor reported. Unlimbering their three howitzers, the Federals demanded an "unconditional and immediate surrender." According to Milam Taylor in a letter to his father that Baylor replied "we would fight a little first."[8]

Following a desultory artillery bombardment, Lynde launched a half-hearted mounted charge. "They commenced firing bombs and grape at us," wrote Taylor, and then "made a charge and advanced within 300 yards of us." Rather than deploying skirmishers to probe the Rebel position and strength, Lynde ordered First Lieutenant Christopher Hely McNally's company of Mounted Rifles to charge through a cornfield, directly into the fire of the concealed Texans. "When close enough for all to get a sure shot the word to fire was given," wrote E. B. D'Hamel of the San Elizario Spy Company. "The first volley emptied about twenty saddles." Although this estimate was an exaggeration, four Federals were killed and McNally and several of his men were severely wounded, and the Mounted Rifles fell back behind their artillery support, "running over the infantry," according to Baylor's report. McKee described Lynde and his staff as "the worst scared men I ever saw. The gray beard and hair of Lynde were a fitting frame for the pale face and cowardly soul."[9]

With the bloody repulse of McNally's horsemen, Lynde, much to the disgust of his officers, ordered a retreat to the fort, which his dispirited column reached at about 10:00 PM. Thinking, perhaps, his victory too easily won, and supposing Lynde's precipitate retreat to be a feint intended to draw him from his position, Baylor did not pursue but held his ground, "expecting that they would attack us under cover of night."[10]

Although McNally, brevetted to captain for his performance in the skirmish at Mesilla, later testified that he considered that "300 men could hold [the fort] against 3000," Fillmore, in fact, had not been designed to withstand a siege. McKee, described the compound as "composed of square adobe houses, with the usual flat roofs, the walls extending up all around, forming a parapet. The officers' quarters on one side, and the soldiers' barracks on two others, formed a quadrangle, enclosing about three acres of ground. The side next to the river was open. The houses were not connected via palisades or earthworks, and were generally twenty or thirty feet apart."[11]

More important from a military point of view, Lynde reported to Colonel Edward R. S. Canby on arriving at his new post that the fort was located in a basin, surrounded by sand hills covered by a dense growth of chaparral. "The sand hills completely command the post," he concluded, "and render it indefensible against a force supplied with artillery. A force of a thousand men could approach within 500 yards under perfect cover." Moreover, water would have to be carried from the Rio Grande, a mile and a half to the west. In addition, the wives and families of five officers, including Lynde's, and those of numerous soldiers—in all about one hundred—were in the fort and of course, subject to injury or death should the Confederates attack. According to the vituperative McKee, Lynde "had been warned repeatedly of this encumbrance" but failed to send his camp followers north to security in Santa Fe.[12]

Capping this list of complications, Lynde felt himself "surrounded by open and secret enemies" and beset by disaffection in his command. The latter of these plaints was much exacerbated when Captains Robert R. Garland and John Marshall Jones "forsook their duties without leave" and defected to the Confederate army, Garland to become colonel of the Sixth Texas Cavalry and Jones to rise to the rank of brigadier general in the Army of Northern Virginia.[13]

When Baylor's scouts observed that the garrison had "dug rifle pits and stretched ropes at the height of a man on horseback on the . . . open side of the post" and were "evidently preparing to defend themselves," the Rebel commander ordered up his artillery and prepared to take the fort by storm. Lynde quickly "became convinced that we must be eventually compelled to surrender if we remained," and that "our only hope of saving the command from capture was in reaching some other military post." He therefore ordered the fort to be evacuated, and "such public property as could not be transported . . . to be destroyed as far as time would allow." At some time between midnight and at 1 o'clock in the morning on July 27, the garrison marched out of the burning fort and into the Organ Mountains. Lynde's hope was that his men would reach water at San Agustín Springs, some 20 miles to the east, by evening and then push on to the safety of Fort Stanton, more than 140 miles away. Some days later Colonel Canby received from Lynde the news that since his unsuccessful attempt to dislodge the Texas troops from Mesilla, "events of the greatest consequence to my command have occurred. They are now prisoners of war."[14]

Shortly after daylight, Baylor had received word at Mesilla of a cloud of dust moving east out of Fillmore. After viewing the retreating Federals through a telescope, he ordered Major Edwin Waller to the fort to extinguish the fire, and with Captain Peter Hardeman's company alone, began the pursuit. "Well," wrote Milam Taylor, "we crowded on in full chase after the brave birds, and about thirty miles from Mesilla we overtook stragglers of the infantry, and disarmed them in squads." McKee later testified that "the day was excessively warm, and there being no water, many men dropped out of the ranks almost dead from fatigue and thirst. . . . Everything was in unalterable and indescribable confusion," McKee testified. "Ruin was on every side of us. The enemy were steadily advancing." Nevertheless, only one man was killed on the retreat. "One brave private, crazed from thirst, fatigue, and undoubtedly despair, fired his musket at Colonel Baylor," said McKee, "and was immediately shot down by him."[15]

The retreating Federals had begun to falter as they approached the steep ascent to San Agustín Pass, and from that point the desert road was strewn with abandoned supplies and equipment. Although his statement has been disputed, Texan cavalryman Hank Smith stated that at least some of the Union soldiers were inebriated. "We began to overtake the infantry scattered along the road in little bunches," he wrote. "We would stack the guns and take all the ammunition. We found some of the guns loaded with whiskey and a good portion of the soldiers drunk and begging for water."[16]

Lynde later reported that he "determined to push forward with a mounted force to the Springs, and return with water for the suffering men in the rear." There, however, he "found the supply of water so small as to be insufficient for my command." Having his men fill as many canteens as possible, Lynde began to make his way back to the main body, but after riding some distance reported that he "became so much exhausted" that he could no longer ride. So he returned to the spring where he established camp, his escort proceeded without him.[17]

Captain Alfred Gibbs of the Mounted Rifles, on his way down to Fillmore from Fort Craig with beef cattle, observed the dust of the marching column and reported to Lynde for orders. The major instructed him to relieve the two companies of the Seventh Infantry that constituted the rear guard. Gibbs found the 150 men of the rear guard, who had marched twenty miles without water, lying beside the road "unable to rise or carry their muskets, and useless and disorganized in every way."[18]

In attempting to check the Rebel pursuit, Gibbs found the road blocked by baggage wagons filled with stores, women, and children. The command's two howitzers were fastened behind the wagons, but Gibbs could find no ammunition for them. He therefore dismounted his seventy lightly armed riflemen and formed a skirmish line at the foot of the hill. Three times, Gibbs reported, he formed his men in line, fell back before superior numbers, and again reformed, all in an effort to at least delay the oncoming Confederates.[19]

At the summit of the pass, the Texans captured Lynde's baggage train and artillery, and for the next five miles, from the summit of the pass to San Agustín Springs where Lynde had established camp, Baylor's men found "fainting, famished soldiers, who threw down their arms . . . and begged for water." When Baylor's men were within two miles of the Federal camp, Gibbs reported to Lynde that Baylor's men were nearly on him and "rapidly advancing." In an apparent state of confusion, Lynde changed Gibbs's orders several times in the next few minutes but then told the mounted men that they could leave for Fort Stanton if they chose. Before Gibbs could mount his command, however, another order instructed him not to move from camp.

When the mounted Confederates—who McKee characterized as a "badly armed . . . irregular command of Texans" and even as "farcical and ludicrous in the extreme"—at last came within three hundred yards of the core of Lynde's exhausted infantrymen, the Federals raised a white flag and asked for terms. Baylor replied that only an unconditional surrender would be accepted, the same terms that Lynde had demanded of him at Mesilla, and Lynde agreed. "Nearly every officer protested earnestly, and even violently, against this base surrender," Gibbs later testified, and McKee stated that "one by one, from the senior down to the junior," Lynde's officers remonstrated with him against surrender, but to no avail. The Confederates took captive between five and six hundred U.S. Army regulars—three companies of the Regiment of Mounted Riflemen, two of the Fifth and six of the Seventh U.S. Infantry—two pieces of artillery, arms and equipment, some two hundred cavalry horses, wagons and their mule teams, and two or three hundred head of beef cattle. Baylor regretted that the colors of the Seventh Infantry "were burned by the enemy to avoid surrendering them." "All surrendered to some 300 Texas militia," McKee complained bitterly, "without firing a shot or losing a single man." Indeed, agreed D'Hamel, "our own force good, bad and indifferent consisted all told of about 280 long eared, ragged Texans." Milam Taylor marveled, "all this was done without a drop of blood lost on our side."[20]

By way of explanation, Lynde reported to Canby, "I considered our case hopeless; that it was worse than useless to resist; that honor did not demand the sacrifice of blood after the terrible suffering that our troops had already under gone, and when that sacrifice would be totally useless." In his own defense, he had little more to say than "My position has been one of great difficulty, and has ended in the misfortune of surrendering my command to the enemy."[21]

Baylor's troops treated their prisoners "with great kindness," Lynde reported, "exerting themselves in carrying water to the famished ones in the rear." Even the vindictive McKee gave the Texans "full credit for humane conduct," reporting that "they were considerate and kind to all, and behaved like soldiers in all respects." Yet it was two days before the infantry could move from the camp, and then only with the assistance of their captors. A few of the prisoners joined the Confederate cause, some chose imprisonment, but most were paroled. To those who chose parole, Baylor issued eighty carbines and food enough to get them through Indian country—across the Journedad del Muerto and up the Rio Grande—to Canby's headquarters at Santa Fe.[22]

"Was there ever such another instance in all history of such imbecility, neglect, or criminal indifference?" the thoroughly outraged McKee rhetorically demanded, but Merrick, if no one else, came to Lynde's defense. He was without the capacity to do proper reconnaissance, Sergeant Merrick said, and was therefore completely fooled as to the true Confederate strength. "That slick old Indian fighter General J. R. Baylor had been maneuvering around Fillmore in such a way as to lead the enemy to think the chaparral full of Texans." The charges against Lynde, he insisted, came "from blatherskites and cowardly citizens that would not shoulder a musket under no circumstances. The howlin curs. Yes, sir; give your enemy the credit due him."[23]

With Lynde's surrender, Baylor's battalion made themselves at home at Fort Fillmore. After the rigors of campaign, the men were happy to find in the area "plenty vegetables and fresh meat," and rejoiced in the fact that "the post has a garden of its own." With their recent success, at least some of Texans thought the campaign was over and sought to go out looking for gold, but Baylor admonished them that "there's Fort Craig and Union in our front. They have to be taken first. After that you may prospect."[24]

The result of Baylor's campaign was, in Confederate secretary of war Judah P. Benjamin's words, "the securing to the Confederacy of a portion of the territory formerly common to all the States but now forming a natural appendage to our Confederate States, opening a pathway to the Pacific and guaranteeing Western Texas from the dangers incident to allowing the Indian tribes in that extensive territory to remain under foreign influence." Benjamin announced to President Jefferson Davis that "official reports" from the field disclosed "the gratifying fact that the population of Arizona is almost unanimously desirous of the annexation of that Territory to the Confederate States." Accordingly, at Mesilla on August 1, 1861, "after satisfying himself of the wishes of the inhabitants," Baylor issued a proclamation organizing that part of the Territory of New Mexico bounded to the north by latitude 36° 30' and to the west by the Colorado River as the Confederate Territory of

Arizona. The seat of government was to be at Mesilla and Baylor was to be governor.[25]

Then, with the U.S. troops having abandoned the the lower Rio Grande, Baylor turned his mind to recruiting new companies from the local population and to dealing with local Indians. In addition to Coopwood's San Elizario Spy Company, two other mounted companies of New Mexico volunteers had taken part in the capture of Fort Fillmore. These units, Benjamin assured the president, had been "furnished by the people, who readily volunteered in our service," and Merrick had no doubt that "there will be other companies formed in the territory as General Baylor is the very man for the business; he will soon make himself popular with the citizens."[26]

The citizens to whom Merrick referred were, of course, white citizens. In organizing a more permanent territorial government for Arizona, Benjamin no doubt spoke for a majority of the South's white citizens when he suggested that "the population is of so mixed a character, and the number of inhabitants educated in representative institutions is so limited, that it would scarcely be practicable to maintain social order and insure the execution of the laws by an elective government," thus effectively excluding the new territory's Hispanic population from the electorate.[27]

Since Baylor's "success in expelling the Federal troops and taking peaceful possession of the Territory," the Secretary of War reported, "an effort has been made by the United States to disturb the tranquility of the inhabitants" by sending an estimated 2,500 men down the Rio Grande under Colonel Canby. Although not marching to attack Baylor, Canby was making every effort to block his movement up the river toward Albuquerque, Santa Fe, and the gold fields of Colorado. In addition to reorganizing the territorial militia, he strengthened the defenses at Fort Craig and removed Fort Union, in the northeastern part of the Territory, from its vulnerable location under a mesa to a new site on the plains, converted it into a fieldwork, and made the officers' and men's quarters bomb-proof.[28]

The garrisons of Fort Buchanan and Fort Breckinridge, which had been marching to reinforce Fort Fillmore, on learning of Lynde's surrender, were diverted to the next link in the line of Union defense along the Rio Grande, Fort Craig. The post had been established by the U.S. Army in 1854 on the west bank of the Rio Grande as protection against Apache raiders. Although Captain Ovando J. Hollister admitted that its adobe walls "would afford no protection against artillery," they were pierced for rifles, and with an adequate garrison it represented a formidable obstacle to the advancing Confederates. Below the fort, the direction from which the Confederates must come, were a series of sand hills crossed by numerous ravines—difficult terrain for an invading army—and opposite the fort, on the river's east side, was a plateau ascending to a steep-sided mesa. "He who would pass up on the east side must go round this, over heavy sand-hills," warned Hollister. The valley above the fort, however, was said to be "wide and beautiful, with considerable timber," providing a convenient invasion route to the north.[29]

Through September and into early October, Baylor sent mounted patrols to probe Fort Craig. These often skirmished with the Union troops, who, Captain George Pettis ruefully admitted, "were usually worsted." On September 18, for example, on a reconnaissance south of Fort Craig, Coopwood's company surprised and captured a company of New Mexico volunteers at the village of Cañada Alamosa. Coopwood paroled the enlisted men after administering a "strong oath," pledging them not to take up arms against the Confederacy but held the Anglo American captain and his Hispanic lieutenant as prisoners. The following evening, Coopwood's men were overtaken by a pursuing force commanded by Captain Robert M. Morris, and in the ensuing firefight Coopwood lost two men killed and eight wounded; Morris reported three wounded. Both forces retreated following the fight.[30]

On September 25, a detachment of the Second Texas Mounted Rifles, commanded by Major Charles Lynn Pyron, attacked the camp of three companies of New Mexico volunteers under a Captain John H. Minks, and according to Merrick, "completely routed them," capturing their "entire outfit" as well as their commander.[31]

3
"1000 Generals": The Army of New Mexico

While these events were playing themselves out on the lower Rio Grande, more than sixteen hundred miles away in Richmond, Virginia, a larger campaign was being planned for the conquest of the entire Southwest. On July 8, 1861, Henry Hopkins Sibley, who had resigned from the U.S. Army in New Mexico Territory on May 13, was commissioned as a brigadier general in the Confederate Army and was authorized to organize a brigade of cavalry in Texas which was to unite with Baylor's battalion, move up the Rio Grande, and "capture the different forts and garrisons in Arizona and New Mexico, and secure the government arms and artillery there."[1]

Sibley persuaded President Jefferson Davis that while serving in the U.S. Army in Arizona he had "acquired full information as to the resources of that Territory and of New Mexico; and as to the condition of the United States forces in those Territories," including their stores, supplies, and transportation, and submitted to him a plan to seize the region. His campaign would be self-sustaining, he assured the president, living off food and material to be captured from Federal forts and depots. Once in control of New Mexico, Sibley intended to enlist an army of

Southern sympathizers who, he was certain, "were anxiously awaiting an opportunity to join the Confederate army," and with them "'On to San Francisco' would be the watchword," and he would blaze a path to the Pacific. California and the Southwest, he reasoned, must become part of the Confederacy, so that the new republic could extend its empire for slavery. Once in firm control of California, New Mexico, Arizona, and Utah, it was but a short step to the annexation of Chihuahua, Sonora, and Baja California, either by purchase or by conquest. "The state of affairs in Mexico," (meaning Benito Juárez's uneasy hold on the Mexican presidency) he pledged, "made it an easy thing."[2]

Military and political authorities, both North and South, were well aware of the instability their southern neighbor's regime and saw Mexico's rich resources as a tempting if forbidden fruit. Colonel James H. Carleton, who was to become commander of Department of New Mexico, considered that it would be a "kind act" to occupy Mexico's northwestern tier of states until a stable central government could properly administer them. He believed that "ethically we have the right, and I doubt very much if it is not our duty to do this." And Colonel James Reily, who Sibley was to send to negotiate with the governors of Chihuahua and Sonora, personally believed that "there are no such mines in the world as are within sight of Chihuahua City," and that "these mines and their soil need the inducement of capital, energy, and enterprise" that, he believed, could be introduced only "by a stable and enlightened constitutional government." Northern Mexico, he averred, "would improve by being under the Confederate flag," and by annexing Sonora and Chihuahua, the South would gain not only their resources but would also be able to construct a railroad from Guaymas to El Paso, thereby rendering Texas "the great highway of nations!"[3]

The overt annexation of Mexican territory does not seem to have been an immediate objective of Sibley's campaign or the policy of the Confederate government. Davis was to refuse Governor Santiago Vidaurri's proffer of Nuevo Léon and Coahuila for annexation in July

James Reily

Reily was born in Hamilton, Ohio, on July 3, 1811, and received a bachelor's degree in 1829 from Miami University, where his father was a trustee. He studied law at Transylvania University in Lexington, Kentucky, and upon admission to the bar, established a practice at Vicksburg, Mississippi, during the summer of 1835. In 1836, he moved to Texas, settling in Nacogdoches and serving as a major in the Army of the Republic of Texas. In partnership with Thomas Jefferson Rusk, the chief justice of the supreme court of the Republic of Texas, Reily moved his offices to Houston. He represented Harris County in the House of Representatives of the Fifth Congress of the Republic, 1840–1841, and in 1842, President Sam Houston appointed him as chargé d'affaires for the Republic in Washington, D.C.

Reily was elected to the House of the Fifth Texas Legislature, 1853–1854, as a Democrat and in 1856, under the administration of James Buchanan, was named U.S. consul to St. Petersburg, but finding the climate not to his liking and the cost of living too high, resigned that same year. On August 20, 1861, he accepted a commission as colonel of the Fourth Texas Mounted Volunteers, with Lieutenant Colonel William R. Scurry as second in command. Reily's first assignment was a diplomatic mission to Chihuahua and Sonora from January through April 1862, and thus he missed his regiment's involvement in the battles of Valverde and Glorieta. He rejoined his regiment and was killed in action at the battle of Camp Bisland on Bayou Teche near Franklin, Louisiana, on April 14, 1864.

1861. Further, in addition to violating Davis's avowed policy of seeking "no conquest, no aggrandizement," such a move would surely have brought a declaration of war from the Juárez government and incurred the displeasure of France and Spain, both at a time when fighting on a single front was increasingly arduous and when Europe's favor was vital to the Confederacy's very survival. Perhaps more important, with Confederate occupation of northern Mexico, the Union navy would have extended its blockade to the ports that were then open and free as international centers of trade for the exportation of Confederate cotton and the importation of arms and ammunition.[4]

But Sibley was most eager to open negotiations with Mexican officials, and acting entirely on his own authority with no sanction from the Confederate government, sent his senior-ranking subordinate, Colonel Reily, commander of the First Texas Mounted Rifles, as a diplomatic agent to the governors of Chihuahua and Sonora. Colonel Tom Green considered him to be "a man of talents as a speaker" but as having "no reputation in Texas as a soldier or officer." The general objective of Reily's mission was to establish cordial and friendly relations between the Confederacy and Mexico and to "counteract any adverse influences, and to obviate any possible objections" to the Confederate enterprise in the Southwest.[5]

Through Reily, Sibley also requested of Governors Luis Terrazas and Ignacio Pesqueira two concessions: permission to purchase supplies and provisions in their states and implementation of a policy whereby Mexican and Confederate troops might cross the international border in "hot pursuit" of Indians. He also had received intelligence to the effect that the Mexican Congress had issued a decree granting the U.S. Army the privilege of moving troops across northern Mexico to attack Texas from the south. Sibley was most eager to learn the veracity of this piece of news and instructed Reily to ask the governors to confirm or deny it.[6]

On January 2, 1862, Reily began the three-hundred-mile journey to Chihuahua City where he met with Governor Terrazas. Following the completion of this mission, he returned to the army to report to Sibley, then headquartered at Fort Thorn, New Mexico Territory, before setting out on his mission to Sonora. At Hermosillo, Reily met with Governor Pesqueira on March 14, 1862. According to Reily, both governors received him cordially and "appeared to be anxious to have the best relations established and continued" between their states and the Confederate States. Both informed Reily that the rumored convention between the United States and Mexico allowing U.S. troops to cross northern Mexico was fallacious, and Terrazas personally assured Reily that "if even the assent of the President had come to him, sanctioned by the act of Congress, he did not think he would permit Federal troops to pass through the territory of Chihuahua to invade Texas." Moreover, both governors were happy to allow the Confederates to purchase all of the supplies in their states for which they were able to pay.[7]

This, of course, fell far short of official recognition, and Terrazas and Pesqueira both declined to accept Sibley's offer of mutual support against hostile Indians, maintaining, in Terrazas's words, that "by that constitutional principle which it is not lawful to violate in any way nor for any consideration whatever," they could not allow the crossing of foreign troops into Mexico. Sibley also proposed that Governor Pesqueira allow the establishment of a Confederate depot at the Pacific coastal city of Guaymas and grant the right of transit from there to El Paso. This, too, the governor politely declined.[8]

Reily's activities in Mexico were reported to the commander of the Department of the Pacific, Brigadier General George Wright, who authorized his subordinate, Colonel James H. Carleton at Fort Yuma, to cross into Sonora should Sibley's forces do so. At the same time, he obliquely warned Governor Pesqueira of "the utter ruin and devastation which would inevitably befall the beautiful State of Sonora should the rebel forces obtain a foothold within its limits," and rather pointedly assured the governor that he had "an army of 10,000 men ready to pass the frontier and protect [the Sonoran] governments and people."[9]

Squeezed between Union and Confederate forces, Pesqueira could only hope to conciliate both and assured Wright that he had nothing but friendly and sincere sympathies for the American Union and hoped that the general could see that through his "cautious management, the chief of the Southern Confederacy could not calculate upon [his] sympathies to carry out his plans." Pesqueira also maintained that any movement of Confederate troops into Sonora would be "considered as an invasion by force of arms." As by this time, Sibley's army was in full retreat, it is not to be wondered at that the Mexican governors would be rethinking their position regarding which side they might favor. "No arrangement or agreement was entered into between the forces or authorities of the States called Confederate and [his] government," Pesqueira assured

Carleton, and further maintained that "the assertions circulated by Mr. Reily" claiming any diplomatic agreement between his administration and the Confederates were "exaggerated, or perhaps badly interpreted."[10]

This diplomatic maneuvering, of course, still lay months in the future when, in July 1861, Sibley "called on all who wanted to volunteer to rendezvous at San Antonio." By the end of October, thirty companies had been recruited, organized into three regiments with three sections of artillery with two mountain howitzers each, sworn in, presented with flags by the ladies of the community, and encamped at Camp Sibley on the Salado River just outside of San Antonio. Private James Franklin Starr of the Fourth Texas Mounted Rifles wrote to his father that the camp ground was "convenient" and boasted "a beautiful drill ground," but the recruits had "not yet been drilled any."[11]

Ten months later, at the end of his first campaign, Starr was to remark that "our *drill* has all been useless." Any attempt to fight a battle using standard West Point tactics "would ruin us," he declared. "Our officers say (or command), 'Come on boys!' and away they go, every man for himself." So loose was their organization that Lieutenant Colonel William R. Scurry of the Fourth Texas was quoted as saying that although he was nominally the commanding officer at the battle of Glorieta, "there were *1000 Generals* in the fight."[12]

The brigade, according to one of their number, "was composed of volunteers from the very flower of the chivalry of Texas" and had enlisted for the war, "fully bent on doing all in their power to carry the Southern Cross to victory, and to make the Confederate States a free, sovereign, and independent nation." Most of the recruits ranged in age from eighteen to twenty-three years and fully expected "to whip the whole United States in time to be home for the Christmas dinner." The brigade's officers were, for the most part, seasoned veterans. Colonel Green, for example, had been a "soldier in all the wars of Texas and the U.S. and C.S. for over 26 years, beginning with San Jacinto." He had served as an artillery officer in the Army of the Republic of Texas and had commanded a company in Brigadier General William Jennings

Worth's division during the Mexican War, seeing heavy action at the battle of Monterrey, and had served as a captain of Texas Rangers, taking part in "many fights with the Comanches" along the western frontier.[13]

The men were required to furnish their own weapons and horses, and although most came in well mounted, their arms consisted mostly of double-barreled shotguns. "They were not considered as army guns," opined Private William Davidson, "but the truth is, just place plenty of courage behind a double-barreled shotgun and it will whip anyone on earth." Some companies had only lances fashioned of carrasco poles. Captain Ovando J. Hollister described the archaic weapons as having a blade three inches wide and twelve inches long, affixed to a nine-foot shaft. "A red guidon was tacked to each where it would drink the blood of a man impaled on it." Sibley assured the men, however, that on arriving in New Mexico they would be furnished with modern arms and equipment out of the Federal supply that they were sure to capture.[14]

For the march across west Texas, each company was furnished with three, six-mule wagons, and Davidson considered Sibley's to be "the most complete and perfectly equipped brigade sent out by the Confederacy during the war."[15]

With the organization complete, however, and everyone eager to start, "we were kept laying around San Antonio for six weeks before we took up the line of march," Davidson complained. Several times orders were issued to move out, but were as often countermanded. Not until November 18, 1861, "after much delay in the preparation for so important a movement," was Sibley ready to move. "At last," wrote Davidson, "we were to have a chance to contribute our share in covering the Confederate arms with glory." He described the brigade as "the finest dressed and equipped body of men that ever left this or any other state." All were well mounted, well armed, and splendidly supplied, "3000 of the noblest sons Texas ever had, all in good health and fine spirits and all the eager for the fray." The long and tiresome march from San Antonio to Fort Bliss, a distance of more than a thousand miles, revealed to Private James H. McLeary of the Fifth Texas Mounted Rifles "the eagerness and determination of the volunteers to meet the enemies of Texas on their own ground and to prevent an invasion of the Lone Star State."[16]

The first detachment of Riley's Fourth Texas Mounted Rifles—a predominately German regiment—left San Antonio for El Paso on October 23, 1861, and the first detachment of Colonel Green's Fifth did not leave until November 10. In the early stages of the march, the men fared well, exchanging coffee for butter, cheese, and milk, but West Texas was brutally barren, and each of the regiments was divided into three battalions, spaced a few days' march apart so that sufficient water and forage might be had for so any horses and men. The route "lay through unbroken wilderness, watered at long intervals," wrote McLeary, and as civilization was left behind, provisions gave out and "we found ourselves obliged to take anything that chanced along." Too often, the men were forced to remain in camp until fresh supplies could be provided.[17]

By early November the men were complaining of marching "through a country where mesquite could not grow, cactus were drying up, and grass and such good things were not to be thought of." One soldier observed that "the natural production of the country is thorns, hills, mountains, & cetera." Such water as the men could find was generally bad, and they were compelled to use weeds and roots for fuel. During the entire march, no rain fell on the brigade, and no forage was available for the horses except for prairie grass. Not surprisingly, when the leading elements of the Sibley Brigade began to arrive at Fort Davis, an oasis in the Davis Mountains of west Texas, on December 2, 1861, at least some of the officers "tanked up considerably."[18]

Not until December 11, 1861, did Sibley, who had stayed behind in San Antonio when the brigade moved out and thus failed to share in the trials of the march, catch up with his men. The less-than-enthusiastic Second Lieutenant Julius Giesecke, recorded in his diary, "we had a grand parade, many good promises made us, etc." At last, by New Year's Day, after what Giesecke called, with considerable understatement, "a wearysome march," the Fifth Texas Cavalry arrived at Fort Bliss, just outside of El Paso. The regiment "had marched 700 miles facing the north wind in the middle of winter. Our teams were worn down until they can hardly walk and our horses were not much better."[19]

Riding now ahead of his brigade, Sibley had arrived at Fort Bliss on December 14 and there assumed command of all the "forces of the Confederate States on the Rio Grande at and above Fort Quitman, and all in the territory of New Mexico and Arizona." Somewhat grandiloquently, he denominated his command the "Army of New Mexico."[20]

Once reassembled, Sibley's regiments proceeded up the Rio Grande at what Milam Taylor characterized as a "very leisurely" pace, aiming to rest and recruit his men and horses. After the Saharan bareness of the West Texas desert, the men found the valley a paradise. William Henry Smith described it as "one of nature's beautiful valleys," at once sublime and "very rich and productive," with "large ranches of stock, such as sheep, hogs &c." But as the brigade approached Fort Thorn, "an old deserted place," the region began to strike the men as more like West Texas than like paradise, and Smith, who had waxed poetical about the area around El Paso, now complained of the scarcity of wood, water, and forage and opined that "this country will be a tax to any government to which it may belong. It is one of the roughest countries that I ever saw or ever expect to see." After only a few days there he reported "some of the boys complaining, some sick, some cooking, some cursing the army, some cursing the Confederacy, some playing cards, some hunting, while others are reading their Bibles."[21]

But while the men were growing bored, Sibley was sending reconnaissance missions "to spy around Fort Craig, to see what the location is and to see how we will manage to attack it." In addition to reporting that "the country around this place is a perfect sand hill," the patrols estimated the Federal garrison to be 2,500 troops. Of those, however, Rebel intelligence sources placed the number of Mexican volunteers at 1,400 men who, according to Smith, "volunteered to fight Indians and not the Southern people. They are badly dissatisfied."[22]

During their first days at Fort Thorn, Sibley's men were "daily and hourly expecting an attack from the enemy," but when Colonel Edward

R. S. Canby did not march out to meet them, the brigade rode north on February 7 to "try the Yankees." Union scouts were out daily, keeping the garrison informed of the gradual Rebel approach. Canby, according to Hollister, was "willing to risk an engagement outside if he could pick his ground," especially as he seems to have believed that Sibley had some field pieces "of range sufficient to batter the post about our ears without coming in reach of our guns." Consequently, on February 13, Canby sent a battalion of infantry to block the Texan's advance at Paradito. The Federals took a strong position in a ravine "and drawed up battle line to fight us," and when it appeared that Sibley intended to attack him there, Canby led out his entire command—"1300 white men, fragments of the Fifth, Seventh and Tenth U.S. Infantry, Co. A, Second Colorado Volunteers, Colonels Piño's and Carson's regiments New Mexican Volunteers and about 300 Rifles and Dragoons," according to Hollister; but the Texans withdrew, and Canby abandoned his line at Paradito and returned to the fort.[23]

"This was wrong," Hollister believed, because the Union position "was so strong that the Texans could not successfully attack it," and they could neither bypass it nor cross the river. "They had but little grub," he maintained, "and in a short time an unconditional surrender would have been the only alternative of starvation." Hollister's generous explanation of Canby's failure to engage the Texans, on this and other occasions, was that the general was confident that he "could corral the whole of them in his own way and time," and so was "determined not to be drawn into a fight except on grounds of his own choice, and not to expose his men when the object could be obtained without it." But with Canby's withdrawal, the Confederates continued their advance, and on February 15, camped in sight of the Stars and Stripes flying over Fort Craig. Major Samuel A. Lockridge, a former filibuster who had served as a senior officer in William Walker's ill-fated Nicaraguan expedition, announced that he intended "to make his wife a shimmy out of that flag and if he can get a wife as easy as he can get that, he will never sleep by himself anymore."[24]

4

"They're Texans. Give Them Hell.": The Battle of Valverde, February 21, 1862

On the day following, the Texans approached the fort "to try the Yankees to see whether they would fight or not," but Colonel Edward R. S. Canby, "having ascertained that their artillery was inferior to ours," declined the gambit and determined to await an attack, and Brigadier General Henry Hopkins Sibley, fearing that the fort was too powerful to take by storm, determined to bypass it, thus disappointing Major Samuel A. Lockridge but no doubt saving the lives of many of his men. Colonel Tom Green later wrote that Sibley "offered General Canby battle under its walls, he declined coming out of the fort on the ground no doubt that he believed we intended then to assault it." Green, who was often in command of the brigade because of a chronic illness that beset the general, claimed that "had Canby come out I intended to charge him and go into the Fort *with him*, pel mel or lose the Brigade." The Confederates could not retreat without giving up all of Lieutenant Colonel John R. Baylor's gains, and

Tom Green

At the time of the New Mexico campaign, Green, in his own words, had been a "soldier in all the wars of Texas and the U.S. and C.S. for over 26 years, beginning with San Jacinto." Born in Buckingham County, Virginia, in 1814, Green moved as a small child with his family to Tennessee in 1817, where in 1834, he graduated from

the University of Tennessee before beginning the study of law with his father, a justice on the Tennessee Supreme Court. At the outbreak of the War for Texas Independence, he rode to Nacogdoches where, in January 1836, he enlisted in the army and was given command of one of the pieces of Texan artillery, the famed "Twin Sisters," which he served at the battle of San Jacinto, winning a battlefield commission from Sam Houston. After rising to the rank of major in the Army of the Republic of Texas, he resigned in May to return to Tennessee to resume his legal studies. He returned to Texas in 1837, however, to become, in turn, a surveyor in Fayette County, engrossing clerk for the House of Representatives of the Republic of Texas, a member of the House of Representatives, secretary of the Senate, and clerk of the state Supreme Court.

Between sessions of the court and the legislature, Green served as a captain of Texas Rangers, taking part in "many fights with the Comanches" along the western frontier as well as in the Republic's desultory war against Mexico, leading a company of volunteers in the campaign to recapture San Antonio in March 1842 and serving as inspector general in the Somervell expedition later that same year. He commanded a company in Colonel John C. Hays's First Texas Mounted Rifles during the war with Mexico, playing a significant role in Zachary Taylor's victory at Monterrey in 1846.

He was elected colonel of the Fifth Texas Volunteer Cavalry, which became part of Brigadier General Henry Hopkins Sibley's Army of New Mexico, which Green commanded at the battle of Valverde in February. The regiment took part in the recapture of Galveston in January 1863, and in the spring of that year Green replaced Sibley in command of the cavalry brigade and took part in the fighting in south Louisiana. He was promoted to brigadier general on May 20 and led his brigade to a succession of victories in south Louisiana, inflicted about three thousand casualties on the Union forces while suffering only six hundred. Elevated to the command of the cavalry division of the Army of Western Louisiana, he played a conspicuous role in Richard Taylor's Red River campaign in April 1864, but on April 12, 1864, he was killed in action at Blair's Landing while leading an attack on Federal gunboats on the Red River.

Green reasoned that "it would have been better to have a risked a battle than to retreat had the enemy come out of the fort."[1]

Fort Craig would not have been an easy nut to crack. As Sergeant Frank Starr, who was later to visit the fort under a flag of truce, reported, it "was very strongly fortified, having a deep wide ditch all around, and port holes for small arms and bastions for artillery." Consequently, on the morning of February 19, Sibley's command marched several miles up the east bank of the river, over country—"a trackless desert of sand," wrote Private James H. McLeary—and camped that night in the sand hills about a mile and a half directly east of and in full view of Fort Craig, "without water for our horses and mules." Surmising that they were attempting to bypass the fort or to plant their artillery on the bluff opposite, it being higher ground than the post, Canby detached a strong force to cross the river on the morning of the nineteenth to hold the high ground and ordered his cavalry and artillery into line, supported at some distance by the infantry, in hopes the Rebels would bring on an engagement.[2]

The Texans, in their turn, hoped that Canby's men, "would come out and give us a fight," and when, shortly before sundown, they saw that "the enemy was drawing up in great force" on the river bank about a mile away, the call to arms was sounded and the brigade drew up in line of battle. The Texans, with "flags flying and the brass band on the little eminence playing 'Dixie,'" awaited a Federal advance. Canby's force, "natives and whites, confident of our superiority, were in the best of spirits and fairly ached for a fight," wrote Captain Ovando J. Hollister. "Skirmishers advanced from both parties, though not far enough to do any harm."[3]

When the Federals came within range, Captain Trevanian T. Teel's Battery opened fire, "breaking their ranks with almost every shot," according to Starr, and "every time the balls fell among the enemy shouts rose from one end of our line to the other." Finding Sibley's position too strong to attack, Canby ordered his artillery and cavalry to return to the fort, "somewhat disappointed, but still in the main reposing every confidence in our chief," and leaving the infantry to watch the Rebels, who "set on a meal of cold bread and dry beef."[4]

No further operations were attempted by either party during the night, with the exception of Captain James "Paddy" Graydon's mule attack on the sleeping camp. Graydon, the former bugler of Captain Richard S. Ewell's Company G, First U.S. Dragoons, and the "enterprising, fearless leader of a desperate band," had been authorized to organize an independent spy company, which, in the words of George Pettis, "would go anywhere their captain would lead them." His men, native New Mexicans, were "recruited from a class that had been despoiled of its all and driven north by the Texans," and in consequence, "they fight from the heart," wrote Captain Hollister.[5]

Shortly after the aborted attack on the Confederate camp, Graydon placed half a dozen 24-pounder howitzer shells, with their fuses cut, into two wooden boxes, which he lashed on the backs of two old mules. Then, with a squad of volunteers from his company, he crossed the river and in the darkness approached the Confederate camp. Within sight of the Texans' horse herd, he lit the fuses, assuming that the unwitting suicide bombers would join the other animals, the shells would explode, and the Rebels would be deprived of their mounts. All went as planned until Graydon and his men, beating a hasty retreat, saw the mules following them back to the Federals' side of the river. The shells did explode, the Confederates were quickly up in arms, and Graydon and his party, frustrated but unscathed, returned to Fort Craig.[6]

Realizing that Sibley was now able to leave Fort Craig on his rear while making a dash for Santa Fe, Canby called together his senior officers and outlined to them his plan to check the Confederate offensive. According to Captain Allen Latham Anderson, Canby intended to closely follow the Rebel march, harassing them "in front, flanks, and rear" with his cavalry while removing or destroying any food and fodder that might fall into Rebel hands and at the same time avoiding a general engagement. The Federal commander had "no confidence in the capacity of the New Mexico volunteers to face the Texans in the open field," but

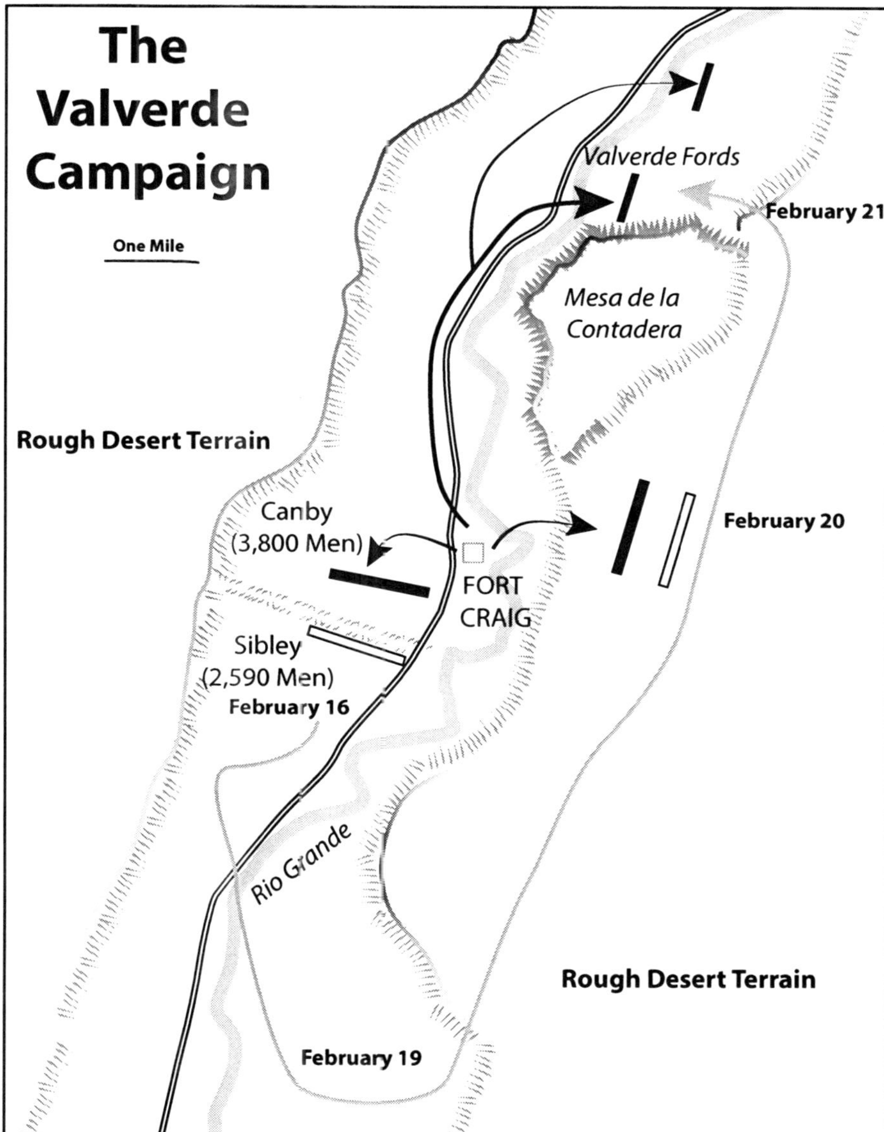

believed that the numerous villages along the Rio Grande would be ideal points at which to carry on a partisan campaign because their adobe walls could be loop-holed and converted into blockhouses, easily defended by

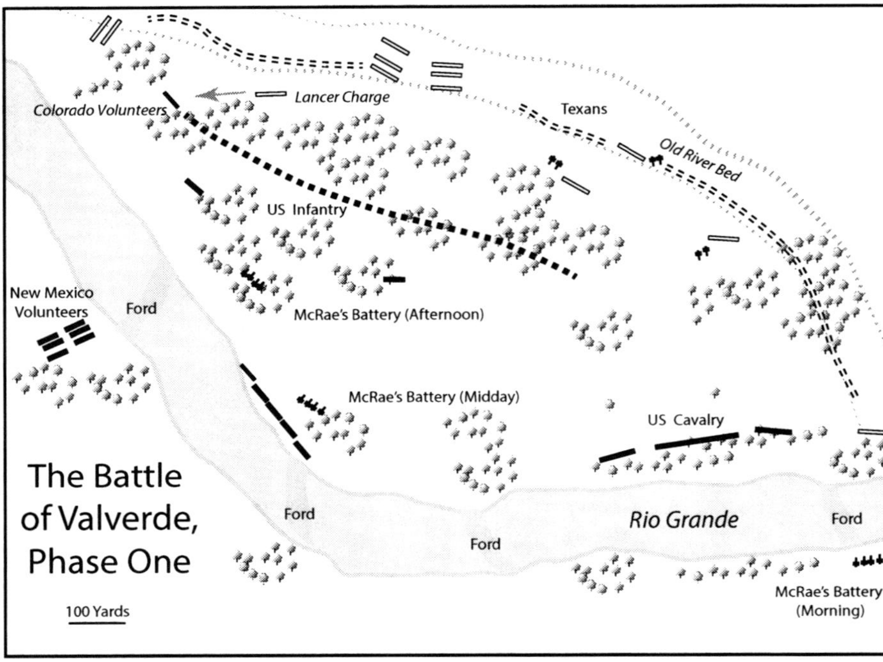

raw troops. Should Sibley refuse to attack these fortified positions south of Albuquerque, Canby planned to unite with the reinforcements coming south from Fort Union, and then take on the Confederates in the open field.

Anderson, one of Canby's staunchest partisans, was not present at this officers' call, but claims to have learned of it from Major Henry Raymond Selden. Whether this was truly Canby's plan, and whether it would have been viable or not, is brought into question by the fact that Canby authorized a set piece engagement on the day following, involving his whole command in what might have been the decisive, all-or-nothing battle for New Mexico. According to Anderson, Canby's plan was marred "by the impetuosity of that rash old fighter," Colonel Benjamin S. Roberts, who aggressively engaged the Rebels at the ford just above Fort Craig, presumably without Canby's approval. This seems improbable, however, given the fact that Canby ordered Roberts to defend the ford at Valverde.[7]

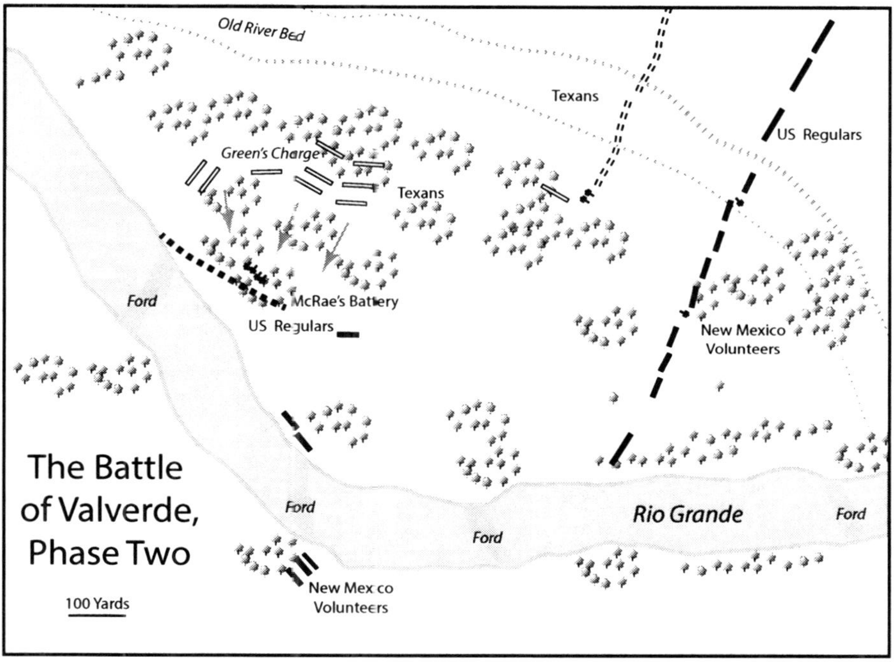

Anderson was unquestionably correct, however, in his assessment that Canby had no confidence in the militia and little in the volunteers. Canby reported that before the Confederates arrived at Fort Craig, he spent "several days" attempting to engage them "in a position where the New Mexican troops would not be obliged to maneuver in the presence of or under fire of the enemy." Unable to bring on such an engagement, believing the fort vulnerable to cannon fire and hoping to block Confederate access to water by denying them one of the few approaches to the river, Canby chose to defend Fort Craig at Valverde, a ford on the Rio Grande seven miles upstream from the fort.[8]

At 5:00 AM on the morning of February 21, a column of Canby's command under Colonel Roberts, consisting of all of his cavalry, Major Robert H. Hall's section of 24-pounder howitzers, two sections of Captain Alexander McRea's battery, one company of the Fifth U.S. Infantry, one company of the Seventh, and two companies of volunteers marched out

Benjamin S. Roberts

Roberts, who Captain Allen Latham Anderson characterized as "that rash old fighter," was a native of Vermont who graduated from the U.S. Military Academy at West Point, graduating fifty-third out of the fifty-six cadets in the class of 1835. After service in the First Dragoons, he resigned his commission in January of 1839 but reentered the army with the start of the Mexican War as a first lieutenant in the Regiment of Mounted Rifles, receiving brevet promotions for every rank through lieutenant colonel for service in the Mexico City campaign.

At the start of the Civil War, Roberts was serving in the Third U.S. Dragoons, but was appointed as colonel of the Fifth New Mexico Infantry with that regiment's formation in December 1861. He received a brevet to colonel for his part in the battle of Valverde, and when his regiment was transferred to the Army of the Potomac at the end of the New Mexico campaign, was brevetted to brigadier general of volunteers for his role in the battle of Cedar Mountain and to major general for his part in the Second Battle of Manassas. He was mustered out of service on January 15, 1866, and died in the District of Columbia on January 29, 1875.

of Fort Craig, making its way north along the valley of the Rio Grande, hoping, as Second Lieutenant Joseph McClellan Bell, commanding a section of Captain Alexander McRae's improvised battery, recalled, "to check the march of the Rebel force towards the upper country."[9]

The morning, which dawned cold and cloudy, found the fourteen hundred-man Confederate column in the saddle on the crest of the ridge overlooking the valley, two miles from the river, with the Mesa de la Contedera lying to the southwest between them and the fort. As Lieutenant Julius Giesecke wrote, they "had neither provisions nor water." Having camped in the sand hills east of Fort Craig, "without water for man or beast," Commissary Sergeant Thomas Benton Collins, Company C, Fifth Texas Cavalry, wrote, "Water we must have."[10]

The morning "brought to us an unhappy state of affairs," agreed Sergeant Starr. The nearest water was five miles away and that way was

Charles Pyron

Pyron was born in Marion County, Alabama, about 1819, but by 1840 was living in Fannin County, Texas. At the outbreak of the Mexican War, he enlisted in Colonel John C. Hays's First Regiment, Texas Mounted Rifles, and took part in the battle of Monterrey. Returning to San Antonio at the war's end, he purchased a ranch on the San Antonio River where he was residing when Governor Edward Clark commissioned him to raise a company of cavalry for state service in March 1861, which he led under Earl Van Dorn at the capture of the Federal forces at San Lucas Springs. On May 23, 1861, Pyron and his men were mustered into Confederate service as Company B, Second Texas Mounted Rifles, and assigned to Brigadier General Henry Hopkins Sibley's Army of New Mexico. Pyron was promoted to major in December 1861, the eve of the campaign, and was assigned to the command of a battalion of Colonel John Robert Baylor's regiment and participated in the battles of Valverde and Glorieta.

Pyron was promoted to lieutenant colonel in command of Baylor's Second Texas Mounted Rifles at the end of the New Mexico campaign, when the regiment was reorganized as the Second or Pyron's Texas Cavalry. He was later promoted to colonel. Pyron died at his San Antonio ranch on August 24, 1869.

over very deep sand. "We were ordered immediately to throw out of the wagons everything but our blankets and clothes," and, after a breakfast of dried beef, Major Charles Pyron, with 150 men of the Second Texas Mounted Rifles, was ordered to take possession of the ford. This detachment was to be followed by five companies of the Fourth Texas under Major Henry W. Raguet, supported by a battery of artillery, with Lieutenant Colonel William R. Scurry, now in command of Colonel James Reily's regiment, to follow.[11]

"At daylight we tried to reach the water," recalled F. S. Wade, a gunner attached to the Fourth Texas's artillery battery, "but the boys in blue were ahead of us and kept us back." At the ford, Pyron's men found themselves confronted by Colonel Roberts's force, which Giesecke estimated as five thousand men and twelve cannon. "It was plainly evident to all the Texans that if they drank water that day, they would have to fight for it." McRae's Battery was immediately ordered, "at a gallop," into position on the west bank of the river, approximately four hundred yards opposite the battery that the Confederates had deployed on the east bank. From a thick grove of cottonwood trees, the superior Federal guns dislodged the Confederate artillery and cleared the left bank of the river "so effectually," Bell wrote, "as to enable the passage of the infantry forces and an occupation of the east bank." By noon, Pettis claimed, "the Confederates had been driven from all the positions they had taken, and were forced to move their guns to a position higher up the river" behind a high drift of sand out of the Union artillery's line of fire.[12]

Pyron "was hard-pressed by heavy forces," wrote Private McLeary, but held his ground until about 10 o'clock when the remainder of the brigade, not exceeding two thousand men, arrived. As the reinforcements moved through the deep sand to the point where the road descended into the valley, the report of cannon was heard in quick succession indicating that the Federal batteries were contesting the crossing. Riding to the sound of the guns, the main body of Confederates entered the valley at a gallop, "hastening on to the fight where the report of musketry announced it to have commenced in earnest."[13]

The men of Raguet's advance guard were "lying down in a little hollow behind a bank which extended several hundred yards from the mesa or hill, towards the river," and the Union line was some six or seven hundred yards beyond, "firing on us with their long range Minnie guns," and the scattering of cottonwood trees that grew near the river was not thick enough to offer cover. "In high spirits and singing songs," the remaining companies of the Fourth Texas under Lieutenant Colonel Scurry descended into the valley to support Raguet and dismounted among the cottonwoods, taking cover behind a slight embankment to his right. As soon as the regiment deployed into line, the Federals greeted it with artillery and small arms fire, "but we were none of us hurt," said Sergeant Alfred B. Peticolas, "as we laid close to the ground and behind the trees."[14]

General Sibley, being euphemistically reported as "quite unwell," remained in the rear, reportedly drunk, and command of the Texans on the field devolved on Colonel Green, who had been left with his regiment to guard the brigade's baggage. Observing Federal reinforcements marching from Fort Craig to the front, however, he moved nearer to the fort to hold in check the infantry and cavalry "pouring out in large force" before marching to the ford, where he arrived between ten o'clock and noon, dismounted his regiment, and posted the Confederates in a dry river bed about eight hundred yards from the Federal line. "I assumed command of the forces on the field being senior present," Green wrote, "expecting every moment to see General Sibley." For four hours, under a heavy artillery fire, the Texans remained busy, digging water wells and shallow trenches in the sand with their Bowie knives, remembered McLeary, and in watching the bursting shells, which for the most part went over them and fell some distance away. Armed to the largest degree with only shotguns, the Texans could not return fire and so "waited anxiously for Teel's artillery to make its appearance, that we might be able to reply to the enemy's artillery."[15]

After lying behind the sand bar for what seemed an interminable time, "listening to the balls whistling over our heads and chatting to one another about the extreme probability of there being a row," five guns of Teel's battery arrived, unlimbering directly in front of Scurry's line. "We tried our howitzers upon them," Starr later wrote to his father, firing at the infantry and artillery across the river, with what Peticolas judged to be "telling effect." The artilleryman, however, "found that the enemy was too far off to do much damage."[16]

The Federal artillery switched its target from the infantry behind the dunes to Teel's guns, "and then we began to feel convinced that we were in a hot place indeed," wrote Peticolas. "Shell and round shot and minie bullets came whistling in showers over our heads, bombs burst just behind and before, and trees were shattered and limbs begin to fall." Counterbattery fire from the heavier Union 24-pounder howitzers disabled one of Teel's guns and the remaining pieces fired until they had expended all of their round shot, then loaded with canister to await an expected Union assault.[17]

While the Federal guns effectively suppressed the Rebel artillery and kept the dismounted cavalrymen firmly pinned behind their sand dunes, Union infantry crossed the river and began advancing through the cottonwoods toward the Confederate line, firing rapidly as they came. When the Yankees were still out of the range of shotguns, most of the Texans could not return fire, but those few who had Enfield rifles "fired upon them with sufficient rapidity to very well reply to their fire."[18]

"Not a man shot without taking sight, for Texas boys are accustomed to the use of arms and never shoot away their ammunition for nothing. Although our balls were not as numerous as theirs, they went with more deadly intent, and our fire soon became extremely galling." The cottonwoods provided only scant protection, and after a firefight that Peticolas estimated about half an hour, the Federals "retreated precipitately towards the river," sped along the way by the fire of Teel's two small howitzers.[19]

The repulse of this Union advance was followed by a lull during which both sides ceased firing and attempted to maneuver into better position. During this interval, the Rebels "suffered very much for water," Peticolas reported, "until some spades were brought up, with which we found water, by digging two or three feet in the bottom of the hollow along which we had our position." Then, for an hour, they remained behind the sand bank, watching the Federals reorganize and redeploy, and Peticolas reported being "surprised and chagrined" by how few men were holding the Rebel front, 250 yards of which was held, as he estimated, by less than one hundred men. By this time, according to Private William Davidson, about fifteen hundred of the Texans had reached the field, facing what he thought to be six thousand Federals supported by six pieces of 6- and 12-pounder artillery and two 10-pounders.[20]

The lull was shattered at about 2:00 o'clock in the afternoon when the Federal artillery opened again, bringing nine pieces to bear on the

Southern line, to which Teel's gunners "could reply but poorly with our four 6-pounders. Our howitzers did not do a great deal of good, being too short and light." The Union infantry, too, began to throw minié balls "thick and close upon our lines." The Confederates could fire only at intervals with inferior weapons, and although "as long as we laid behind the sand banks our own lives were in comparative safety," every few moments a Texan would be killed or wounded.

Canby reached the field at 2:45 PM, relieved Roberts and, under a heavy artillery barrage, crossed the river with McRea's battery, supported by two companies of the Fifth and Seventh Infantries, and two companies of the Second Colorado Infantry—"Pike's Peakers," to the respectful Texans. Colonel Kit Carson's First New Mexico Infantry was held in reserve. East of the river, Canby's men "took position in front of us . . . at a distance of 600 yards," Green reported, and at about 3:00 o'clock by his reckoning, three or four hundred riflemen (Captain Theodore H. Dodd's company of Colorado Volunteers, according to some sources) opened "a most galling fire" on Scurry's regiment, anchoring the Confederate right. "Now," said Peticolas, "I began to feel almost disheartened." The Texans "made a desperate resistance," wrote Rebel Private Wade, but "were pushed back and back," and the Federal artillery advancing on the Confederate right threatened to unlimber in a position that could enfilade the line of dismounted cavalry behind the sand dunes. "In two minutes," Peticolas feared, "a raking fire up our line on the side of the bank would slay the last man of us."[21]

"Everything looked gloomy," Green later wrote. "Nothing but a *desperate* effort could save us from annihilation." To suppress the fire on his right, Green ordered a mounted charge against the Federal left, only to countermand the order a few minutes later. Captain Willis Lang's company of some forty lancers failed to hear the counter command, however, and in what Green characterized as "one of the most gallant and furious charges . . . ever witnessed," briefly broke through the Federal line. Company A of the Second Colorado, on the extreme left flank of the Union line, was at first under the mistaken impression that the lancers were friendly cavalry, but as they approached at the charge the captain called out, "They're Texans. Give them hell."[22]

According to the Colorado miners, the lancers "looked as if the Devil had set them on the end," but as they were armed with only lances, the rifles of the Pike's Peak regiment easily drove them back, "for the boys could not use those long lances, as the limbs of the great cottonwood trees were in their way." In the Quixotic charge, Lang was mortally wounded and his company decimated. Green claimed, however, that "the enemy was repulsed, and our right was for some time unmolested."[23]

Shortly afterward, Green ordered a second mounted charge—this by 250 men of the Fourth and Fifth regiments under Major Raguet—against Hall's two 24-pounder howitzers and their supports on his left flank near the foot of the Mesa de la Contedera or Black Mesa, as the men called it. According to Lieutenant Colonel Andrew W. Evans's account, Canby had personally sited Hall's battery on the extreme right of the Union line, a mile downstream from McRae's, and had directed the placement of its supporting troops—Captains David Brotherton's and Benjamin Wingate's companies of the Fifth U.S. Infantry, Major Thomas Duncan's battalion of the Third U.S. Cavalry, and Carson's New Mexico infantry. Raguet's attack, he wrote, was a complete surprise and the attacking force outnumbered the battery's supporting infantry, which "had hardly—if at all—got completely into position when the Texan charge was made."[24]

The attack was repulsed, although Green admitted that "our little body of cavalry could make no impression on the enemy," like Lang's, it pulled heavy bodies of infantry out of the center of the Federal line to the support of the guns on its flanks. As Private Wade wrote, "we could see detachments leave the center to reinforce that point." Lieutenant Bell, commanding a section of McRae's guns, agreed that Lang's and Raguet's threats to the Union flanks had "commanded the attention of our infantry supports," resulting in their shifts to left and right, leaving the center dangerously thin. This realignment brought about the climax of the battle.[25]

Just as the broken survivors of Raguet's forlorn hope were drifting from the field, Green launched a general assault, with devastating results.

Although believing himself to be vastly outnumbered, Green professed to have "the most unbounded confidence in the courage of [his] troops," and ordered a general assault against the thinned Union center. Major Lockridge, Green's chief of staff, came riding down the line yelling: "Charge 'em! Damn 'em, charge, charge, charge!" Wade described how the Texans "leaped out from behind the sand dunes, not like pictures of charges in the books, but like a lot of school boys, yelling at the top of our voices and charging at full speed." Lieutenant Bell saw the Texans rise from the old river bed and surge forward. "Wild disorder and determination were the moving features."[26]

The distance between the two lines was some eight hundred yards of open terrain, but "on they came," Bell recorded—only two hundred according to Peticolas, "about 750 on the ground," Green reported, and "some 12 or 1500 men" according to Bell's estimate—"without order, each man for himself, and the 'devil for the vanquished,' in true 'Ranger' style, down to almost the muzzles of our guns." The Federal infantry "fired by platoons, but I reckon they were scared, for the cottonwood limbs rattled down on us, but not one of our boys was hit." The Federal cannon, whose tubes were elevated to fire at long range, shot over the heads of the charging Rebels. The guns were supplied with only round shot and spherical case rather than grape. Private Henry C. Wright stated that the Texan volunteers, "although new to battle, were old in strategy." Each man, he said, watched for the flash of the artillery and threw themselves on the ground as the shot passed over, then rose and pushed forward again. "No wonder they thought we fell in hundreds."[27]

Even so, wrote Sergeant Starr, "the scene was terrible, the balls were whistling around as thick as a hail, but we had by this time got used to that." In the ensuing hand-to-hand conflict, the Southerners' double-barreled shotguns and revolvers, which had until then had been virtually useless because of their short range, were employed to great advantage. When within fifty yards of the Union line the shotguns of the charging Texans, hunters all, "mowed the poor boys down by the hundreds," Wade claimed. The Colorado volunteers, deployed in support of Hall's guns, came in for particularly heavy fire, and "it

Christopher "Kit" Carson

Carson was born in Madison County, Kentucky, on December 24, 1809, but before he was two years old his family moved to Missouri where he spent most of his youth. At age fourteen, Carson was apprenticed to a saddle maker but later ran away and joined a wagon train headed west to Santa Fe, New Mexico, where he became a

fur trapper. In 1846, John C. Frémont hired Carson as a guide and hunter on his California expedition, and with the outbreak of the Mexican War he was commissioned a second lieutenant in Frémont's impromptu California Battalion. In September, Frémont dispatched Carson to Washington, D.C., to brief officials on the situation in California, but in New Mexico, he encountered Brigadier General Stephen Watts Kearney's Army of the West and was ordered to guide it to California where he was instrumental in extricating it from the siege of Californio partisans following the battle of San Pasqual, fought near San Diego on December 6, 1846.

In May 1847, Carson at last arrived in Washington, D.C., where President James K. Polk commissioned him a second lieutenant in the Regiment of Mounted Rifles, but his commission was revoked by the Congress.

After the war, Carson worked as a trapper and scout and served as an agent for the Ute Indians from 1854 to 1861. With the outbreak of the Civil War, Carson was commissioned colonel of the First New Mexico Infantry, leading his regiment at the battle of Valverde. Tasked with the removal of Apaches and Navajos from their ancestral lands to reservations, in July 1863, Carson began a devastating campaign against American Indians. By the end of January 1864, between six and eight thousand Navajos had been removed to the Bosque Redondo. The long march to the remote reservation resulted in many Navajo deaths. For this service, in March 1865, Carson was brevetted as a brigadier general. Carson left the army in November 1867 and died near Fort Lyon, Colorado, on May 23, 1868.

was here," wrote Private Wright, "that the brave Pikes Peak men met their fate." The regulars also fought bravely, he recalled, "but volleys of musketry do not count much when opposed to men accustomed to taking dead aim at individual marks."[28]

The volunteer regiments quickly evaporated, however, dropped their rifles, abandoned their artillery, and plunged into the shoulder deep river,

Alexander McRae

McRae, a North Carolina native and a member of the West Point class of 1847, was commissioned as a second lieutenant of the Regiment of Mounted rifles and by 1861 had been promoted to captain in the regiment, which by then had been redesignated as the Third U.S. Cavalry. Placed in temporary command of a battery of artillery, he was killed in the defense of those guns the guns at the battle of Valverde, February 21, 1862.

Samuel A. Lockridge

Lockridge was born in 1829, but by the late 1840s and early 1850s, he was living in Cincinnati, Ohio, where he was a partner in the merchant firm of Smith and Kissane, and was known as William Kissane. In January 1852, Kissane took out an insurance policy on the steamship *Martha Washington* and its cargo. When the ship, its cargo, and some sixteen people aboard it burned shortly thereafter, Kissane was charged with its destruction and fled to Texas to become Samuel A. Lockridge. In 1856, Lockridge recruited and organized 283 "Texas Rangers" who he led with the rank of colonel in William Walker's filibustering expedition to Nicaragua. He returned to Texas in August 1857 to recruit reinforcements from the ranks of the Knights of the Golden Circle, but after a disagreement with Walker, he abandoned the cause. With the organization of Brigadier General Henry Hopkins Sibley's Army of New Mexico, Lockridge was commissioned as the major of the Fifth Texas Cavalry. He was killed in action at the battle of Valverde in the assault on Alexander McRae's battery.

which was running with ice. "Our New Mexican allies," as soon as they came under fire, Bell observed, "fled to a more secure position on the west bank of the river; nor did they rest there, but continued their flight to still more distant quarters," abandoning Carson and a few of his officers. Green also noted that the volunteers "were not made of as good stuff as the regulars," reporting that "a few fires upon them with their own artillery and Teel's guns, a few volleys of small arms, and the old Texas war shout completely dispersed them."[29]

The Texans followed, "yelling like so many Indians." At the river, the routed Union troops "were mowed down, the water being covered with their dead bodies." The fugitives almost choked the ford, thus, according to Wright, blocking the Confederate pursuit. "We stood on the bank and fill the river with dead men." Although Confederate letters and diaries universally report that "the mortality amongst them in the river was terrible," Federal sources claim that no more than a dozen of Canby's men were killed in crossing the Rio Grande, and probably that many more were wounded.[30]

On the Union right, Hall's battery was able to limber its guns and escape across the river, its retreat covered by the cavalry. On the Union left, however, McRae's Battery, despite being held with a determination that McLeary characterized as "hardly less heroic than the charge of the victors"—losing more than one-half of its gunners in a hand-to-hand fight with revolvers, clubbed rifles, and sponge staffs—was overrun and all but two guns and three caissons were captured. Its supporting troops—who had just repulsed Raguet's charge—"gave way with little resistance and fled in utmost confusion." McRae, a North Carolina native and a member of the West Point class of 1847, was killed at the guns. Major Lockridge led the charge, and as he approached the battery, McRae was standing at one of the guns, his hand upon the knob of the cascabel. Lockridge, according to Pettis's account, placed his hand on the muzzle of the piece and called for McRae's surrender. Standing no more than three feet apart, both raised their revolvers and fired, killing each other instantly.[31]

Desperately hoping to reverse this sudden change of fortune, Canby ordered his reserve cavalry to recapture McRae's battery and to hold it until the Fifth Infantry could come to its support. Although the charge was made "with the best intentions," it was "not a success," Bell ruefully admitted, and "seems to have changed the whole spirit of the fight." The charge, he wrote, "only succeeded to some extent in covering the retreat of the infantry, many of whom perished in crossing the river." Far blunter was Captain Hollister, who claimed that Captain Richard S. C. Lord of the First Dragoons "would not raise a finger to prevent the battery from being taken, and when ordered to charge the enemy after its capture," after starting toward the melee, wheeled his company about, "turned tail and fled from the field."[32]

The numerous errors of fact in Sergeant John William Ellis's account of the battle of Valverde render his testimony suspect, but he was certainly angriest, if not most accurate, in his insistence that Captain Henry Raymond Selden and the Fifth U.S. Infantry "made repeated charges" in an effort to retake McRae's Battery, despite Canby's direct orders that he retire from the field. Most damning, if true, is his charge that Ellis's company commander, Captain Wingate, having been carried to the post infirmary when his leg was shattered by a cannonball, confronted Canby after the battle with the dramatic last words: "Leave me. You are a traitor. Could I but live to get to Washington!"[33]

"I thought that I had experienced a good many moments of exquisite pleasure," remembered Peticolas, "but never before have I felt such perfect happiness as I did when we took the battery from our enemy." The captured guns were manned by the Confederates, faced about, and poured their fire into the retreating Federals. At this point, Canby gave the somewhat redundant order to withdraw, reportedly calling to his men, "Retreat to the fort! Every man escape as best he can." The Federals "fled from the field, both cavalry and infantry, in the utmost disorder," Green boasted, "many of them dropping their guns to lighten their heels, and stopping only under the walls of the fort. Our victory was complete." Scurry, with a body of mounted men, pursued the fugitives across the river but was recalled—"why I have never learned," wrote Starr, but "as our boys all came along and gathered along the bank of the river, yell after yell went up, which could have been heard for miles around."[34]

The retreat, Hollister admitted, "was somewhat disorderly at first," but as the Confederates mounted no pursuit the Federals rallied and reached Fort Craig in good order. The road, however, was strewn with arms and baggage, and Private Wright believed that "had we been in condition to do so," the Confederates could easily have taken the fort and captured Canby's whole command. Indeed, for two days after the battle, Wright believed, "the fort would have surrendered had we demanded it." McLeary, who characterized the Federals' retreat as "almost a rout," also believed that "had it been closely followed up the fort might have been captured." But the Texans, as disorganized in victory as the Federals were in defeat, were nevertheless dismayed when General Sibley, having recovered from his indisposition, appeared on the field at 7:00 PM, "stood up, took command, and ordered no advance on the retreating army." Canby fully anticipated that the Confederates would exploit their victory on the field by an assault on the fort that night, but Bell insisted the roughly used garrison was quickly "put into shape to resist any attack that might be made upon the fort." So, with Fort Craig still seven miles distant, the firing ceased and night came on to close the carnage. The Confederates camped on the river that night "in strange confusion," their regiments in a promiscuous mix but well supplied with food from captured haversacks and having "obtained water in plenty, but with the cost of blood."[35]

The numbers of men engaged on both sides and the losses that both incurred and inflicted at Valverde are a matter of dispute. Sergeant Starr reported that the Confederate force of the field did not exceed 1,200 men, and Sibley's official report claimed that his force was not more than 1,750. Pettis estimated the Confederate column to number "about two thousand men." Sibley, in no condition to judge, estimated the Federal force at 4,000 to 5,000.[36]

Peticolas's estimate of Union losses at "about 350 killed and 400 wounded" was also greatly overstated. Canby reported a loss of 3 officers and 65 men killed, 161 wounded, and 1 officer and 34 men captured. Seventeen of the wounded later died. Green reported the Confederate loss at 41 killed, 145 wounded, and one missing, but among the dead were two field grade officers, Lockridge and Lieutenant Colonel John Schuyler Sutton of the Seventh Texas Mounted Rifles.

The respect that the combatants showed for one another is in marked contrast to the bitter hatred that evolved later in the war, with the Texans and the Colorado volunteers feeling a special bond. "Not one of these boys but would have divided his last crust with us or we with him," Private Wright noted with grim irony, "but all day long on the 21st of February, 1862, we murdered one another."[27]

The six pieces of artillery that the Confederates captured from McRae's Battery were placed under the command of First Lieutenant Joseph Draper Sayers, former adjutant of the Fifth Texas Cavalry and future Texas governor, and dubbed the "Val Verde Battery." Additionally, the Rebels captured about three hundred Springfield rifles, which replaced shotguns and hunting rifles, a considerable quantity of ammunition, a number of revolvers, and "a considerable number of castoff overcoats." Especially welcome to the Rebels, who had for days been faring on dried beef, were the contents of the captured Federal haversacks: three days' rations of "light bread, coffee, sugar, and bacon."[38]

Following the battle, Canby—who received a brevet promotion to brigadier general of volunteers for "gallant and meritorious service" at Valverde—was roundly excoriated by his officers and men, first for staying away through the early stages of the battle and then for botching what Roberts had well begun, and particularly his ill-advised crossing of the river—thus placing his guns within reach of a Rebel charge—for the Federal debacle at Valverde. "It will be observed that while Colonel Roberts was in command of the Union troops everything was moving in their favor," wrote Captain Pettis, "but when Canby assumed command the tide of battle turned, until finally the Union forces were beaten and in retreat." Sergeant Ellis, a veteran of the Fifth U.S. Infantry, testified that the battle of Valverde was "well and valiantly fought, while Colonel Roberts . . . was in command," and the nearly unanimous opinion of the officers engaged was that if Canby had remained at Fort Craig, the Confederates would have been forced to retreat to San Antonio.[39]

Canby himself cast the blame on Colonel Miguel Estanislado Piño's Second New Mexico Infantry. "The battle was fought almost entirely by the regular troops with no assistance from the militia and but little from the volunteers, who would not obey orders, or obeyed them too late to be of any service," he complained bitterly to Adjutant General Lorenzo Thomas. The fact that large numbers of the New Mexican volunteers deserted his ranks during and after the battle, Canby added bitterly, "adds to rather than diminishes our strength." His partisan, Allen Latham Anderson, also blamed the Union debacle on the New Mexican volunteers, who remained under the shelter of the river bank and refused to move forward to fill the gap in the center of the Union line when the Confederates attacked. "For this, of course, Canby was not responsible." According to Confederate sources, the New Mexico volunteers "were highly demoralized," even before the battle, "and did not want to fight," and many deserted in a panic "caused by their first meeting with the Texans," who, they reportedly said, "fought not like men but like devils." Piño's regiment deserted after the battle, and numbers of other New Mexicans fled, not to the fort, but from it, leaving "the living to suffer, the wounded to die," noted Peticolas.[40]

Lieutenant Colonel Evans maintained, as well, that because "the Union troops were successful in the morning under Colonel Roberts and were defeated in the evening under Colonel Canby was the fortune of war. It is not always correct to argue post hoc, propter hoc. The result would probably have been the same if the commanders had been reversed, or if Colonel Canby had remained at Fort Craig." Hollister was of the opinion that although Canby was guilty of having failed to respect "the audacity and effectiveness" of his opponents and to have "given his personal attention to the details of the business," he had incurred "the suspicions of the ignorant and thoughtless" through no fault of his own. Rather, "the impatience of subordinate officers" and the behavior of "cowards and traitors who would not stand by him on the field," had prevented him from trapping the Army of New Mexico east of the Rio Grande.[41]

While Canby was being castigated for his leadership, or lack thereof, at Valverde, the Texans were quietly muttering among themselves about Sibley's apparently drunken condition, his absence from the battlefield, and his squandering of the victory that his men had won under Green. "The battle of Valverde ought to have settled the question of the conquest of New Mexico by 7 o'clock of the same night," insisted Captain William Lee Alexander of the Fourth Texas Mounted Rifles. Were it not for Sibley's interference, he was convinced, the Texans could have taken Fort Craig without the loss of another man. "The enemy were totally routed and scattered and all we had to do was to *push on* and the fort was ours." Instead, the victorious Confederates were ordered to halt "just as we had them all in a good run." Whoever was to credit or blame for the result of the battle, the Texans had won a significant victory and as Private Wright observed, "now had no obstruction to our onward march." But from that point onward, Sibley's defects as a commander were to become increasingly evident.[42]

5

"Starvation seems to stare us in the face.": The Glorieta Campaign, February 22–April 2, 1862

On the day after the battle, February 22, the twenty-sixth anniversary of the beginning of the siege of the Alamo, Brigadier General Henry Hopkins Sibley sent Lieutenant Colonel William R. Scurry and Captain Denman William Shannon to demand of the surrender of Fort Craig. Although Colonel Edward R. S. Canby agreed to an exchange of prisoners and a truce to bury the dead, he refused to surrender. This left the Texan commander in a serious dilemma. Although they had won a tactical victory at Valverde, his men had only about five days' rations. He was faced with the choice of retiring to the Mesilla Valley or continuing north with the hope of capturing Federal supplies at Albuquerque, Santa Fe, and Fort Union, but leaving a strong enemy garrison on his rear. As long as Canby held Fort Craig, the Confederate line of communications

The Campaign for New Mexico
50 Miles
SANGRE de CRISTO MOUNTAINS
Taos
FORT UNION
Santa Fe
Glorieta Pass
Las Vegas
Galisteo
SANDIA MOUNTAINS
Bernal
Albuquerque
GLORIETA MESA
Pecos River
Rio Puerco
Peralta
MANZANO MOUNTAINS
Rio Grande
NEW MEXICO TERRITORY
MAGDALENA MOUNTAINS
Socorro
SAN MATEO MOUNTAINS
FORT CRAIG
Jornada del Muerte
SAN ANDREAS MOUNTAINS
CONFEDERATE ARIZONA
FORT THORN
Doña Ana
Las Cruces
Mesilla
ORGAN MOUNTAINS
Franklin
MEXICO
El Paso del Norte
FORT BLISS

was interdicted, and the garrison there presented a constant threat to the Confederate rear.

At noon on February 23, the Army of New Mexico, its commander "not considering it best to storm a fort so well fortified" and believing that Canby "would be obliged to eventually to surrender it or evacuate," abandoned a number of its wagons for want of teams, burned saddles, and old clothes and took up the line of march for Santa Fe. Unfortunately for the Southern cause, after wasting two full days before setting out, the Sibley Brigade "laid in camp" on the twenty-fourth while "the quartermasters were busy dividing out the plunder that had been confiscated." At that moment, many in the army believed, "a party of 500 men might have been sent up the river with dispatch and taken the *entire* Territory including Fort Union."[1]

Although, in fact, some 800 U.S. Regulars and New Mexico volunteers then held Fort Union, with the First Colorado Volunteers ready to march from Denver, the Confederates believed that not more than 250 Federals then occupied the northern part of the territory, and Sergeant Frank Starr believed that "a body of 600 men well mounted," could have taken possession of Albuquerque, Santa Fe, and Fort Union. When, after a week of delay, Major Charles Pyron's command was sent to take possession of the Federal stores only one hundred miles up the river, it was already too late because by the time it arrived at Albuquerque, the principal army depot for the territory, the hay had been burned and the commissary and quartermaster buildings were on fire. According to an eyewitness report by Spruce M. Baird, who had been sent to New Mexico as a county judge when the Republic of Texas still claimed the area, Captain Herbert M Enos "burned everything they had" at Albuquerque—"enough to last the whole brigade six months"—and then retired toward Santa Fe."[2]

On March 4, Major James Lowry Donaldson, the quartermaster at Santa Fe, destroyed the government stores there and fell back with the territorial government to Fort Union. Although Pyron's battalion was able to salvage a considerable quantity of supplies from the flames, an abundance was lost. "A quick moment on our part would have put us in possession of it all," Captain William Lee Alexander complained, but "such was our *masterly* inactivity, that a large reinforcement from Denver City came in and so we got neither Fort Craig nor Fort Union, and at Fort Union I am satisfied we would have found rations sufficient to last the brigade 12 months and an immense amount of other public property."[3]

By the coming of spring, the men of the Sibley Brigade would bitterly regret that their general had "acted so recklessly as he did after the battle of Val Verde in not sending a force of five or 600 men on the best horses straight onto [Albuquerque] to prevent the enemy from destroying everything." Had he done so, Alfred B. Peticolas lamented, they would have had "two or three months' provisions for the whole brigade, for at least that much was destroyed here by the Ab[olitionist]s, who hurried up directly after the battle for the express purpose of destroying it." Although the Confederates, as Lieutenant Julius Giesecke observed, "were not troubled by the enemy anymore," their occupation of the upper Rio Grande became but a hollow victory.[4]

In addition to these portentous difficulties farther up the Rio Grande, Sibley's column was experiencing serious troubles on its rear. New Mexico Territory was the home to numerous tribes of American Indians, and of those tribes—including the warlike Kiowas, Comanches, and Navajos—the Mescalero Apaches were most problematic to white settlers, whether their allegiance was to the North or the South. Their perpetual raids and ambushes conducted against soldiers and civilians from the first Spanish settlement in the area in 1598 were, as Private James H. McLeary wrote, "instigated only by love of plunder and not from any desire to take part in the Civil War."[5]

On March 20, 1862, Lieutenant Colonel John R. Baylor, an inveterate Indian-hater, issued an order to Captain Thomas Helm, who was guarding the Pinos Altos mines, to "use all means to persuade the Apaches or any tribe to come in for the purpose of making peace, and when you get them together, kill all the grown Indians and take the children prisoners and sell them to defray the expense of killing the Indians." Baylor, according to according to John B. Jones, a war department clerk, justified this slaughter on the grounds that genocide was "the only mode of dealing with such savages." According to Baylor, "the Apaches murdered our people invited to make a treaty with them"; his intention, therefore, was "to retaliate by extermination of them."[6]

A few months later Baylor and Confederate commissioner James McCarthy attempted to negotiate with the Mescalero Apaches, offering them rations, blankets, and employment as scouts for the Confederate army in exchange for peace. Chief Nicholas, meeting with the Confederate authorities at El Paso on August 7, told the peace commissioners "My heart is full of love for my pale-face brothers. They have not spoken with forked tongues. We have made a treaty of peace and friendship. When I lie down at night the treaty will be in my heart, and when I arise in the morning it will still be there. And I will be glad I am at peace with my pale-face brothers."[7]

On his return trip to Fort Davis, however, Nicholas seized the revolver of a fellow passenger and jumped from the stagecoach, to return the following day with his warriors to kill two guards and drive off most of the garrison's horses. Baylor sent a fourteen-man detachment under Lieutenant Reuben E. Mays in pursuit, and on August 10, the Texans overtook the raiders and recovered about one hundred head of horses. Rather than return to the fort, however, Mays's men pressed the chase, again overtaking the Mescalero Apaches later in the day. This time, however, the Indians were well-posted in a narrow, rocky canyon. The Confederates were eager for a fight, and so Mays, who Merrick characterized as "a novice in Indian warfare," ordered an attack. The charge was met by an intense fire from Nicholas's one hundred warriors, and in less than ten minutes Mays and all but one of his men had been killed.[8]

Secretary of War Judah P. Benjamin reported that "all the proceedings of Lieutenant-Colonel Baylor appear to have been marked by prudence, energy, and sagacity, and to be deserving of high praise," and on December 15, 1861, he was promoted to colonel. He resented being superseded in command, however, reporting that "the goodwill of the people of the territory he had gained was being destroyed by the actions of Sibley's troops." His popularity was eroded when he mortally wounded Robert P. Kelley, the editor of the Mesilla *Times*, in a duel, and when Secretary of War George Wythe Randolph referred his notorious extermination order to Jefferson Davis, the end to Baylor's career in New Mexico came quickly. "He cannot sanction such a perfidious crime," John B. Jones, a clerk in the Confederate war department, said in his diary. To his credit, Davis characterized Baylor's report as "a confession of an infamous crime," and removed him from civil and military command.[9]

The march up the Rio Grande began auspiciously enough. Seemingly corroborating Captain Allen Latham Anderson's account of Canby's plan to carry on a scorched earth campaign should the Confederates bypass Fort Craig, on the night of February 22, Canby ordered the New Mexican militia to march north, hoping, he said, that they would impede Sibley's operations by "obstructing his movements, cutting his supplies, removing from his route the cattle, grain and other a supplies in private hands that would aid him in sustaining his force." Instead, as territorial governor Henry Connelly wrote, "the militia have all disbursed and have gone to preparing their lands for the coming harvest, and that is by far the best use that could be made of them."[10]

Although Peticolas complained that wood was extremely scarce and "the grass is not worth a straw for horses," the brigade reached Socorro on February 26, "and as soon as they had thrown a cannonball into the town, the white flag announced that they had surrendered." The Rebels bagged some two hundred New Mexican volunteers as prisoners, three hundred stand of arms, some three hundred horses and mules, eight thousand barrels of flower, and a number of wagons.[11]

Despite the capture of a large herd of horses and mules at Socorro, losses at Valverde and the lack of forage—"either corn, hay, or grass," Peticolas lamented, "and it grows scarcer as we approach Santa Fe"—led the Fourth Cavalry to give up its horses on February 27 and from then on served as infantry. Although Peticolas insisted that "the idea is not as repugnant to them as one would naturally suppose it would be to the cowboy of Texas," Sergeant Theophilus Noel reported that "the regiment is more depressed than it has been for months." Private Henry C. Wright complained, "Our officers glibly assured us that if we would consent to this measure that as soon as we returned to Texas we would be remounted at the expense of the government, and as our horses were likely to die anyhow, it would be a wise thing for us to get rid of them now. All this sounded very nice, but I noticed that Colonel [Tom] Green's men did not give up their horses, neither did they die but recruited from the best of ours they rode through the campaign and back to Texas, while we footed it all the way and had to remount ourselves again at home."[12]

On February 28, leaving his sick and wounded in a makeshift hospital in Socorro, Sibley moved on, the dismounted "mounted rifles" taking their first march as infantry, and Noel reported, "many a foot was blistered." Pressing on toward Albuquerque, Peticolas complained that "we are now beginning to experience about the greatest of the manifold hardships of war." Only two days north of Socorro, he noted that "we have been a day without bread, and there is no more bread stuff in the train." The misery of growing hunger was compounded by the bitter cold, the deep sand, and the fact that the men had only buffalo chips for fuel. On the battlefield, he reasoned, with "the fierce din of conflict and the danger to face," courage and convictions sustained the men, "but to trudge along day after day with nothing to eat save beans, with no teams to transport our baggage, and no forage," and to "feel the weakness and gnawing of hunger . . . is a feature of soldiering without any redeeming trait." Peticolas was scarcely understating the case when he wrote on March 5, "For such green volunteers, scarce three months from all the comforts of a home life in an enlightened country, we have had pretty rough experiences."[13]

Through the first days of March, the men of the Army of New Mexico grew increasingly disillusioned with the object of their conquest. "The country is unfit for any use at all," groused Private William H. Smith. "This country never was intended for white folks. The first man ever came to the country ought to have been killed by the Indians."

Nevertheless, he declared the men "willing to live on beef, poor as it is, to accomplish our object."[14]

So dire had the situation become by March 5 that Sibley held a council "to ascertain the feelings of the officers whether they were willing to travel on or not." According to Private Smith, the majority were opposed continuing the campaign. "Starvation seems to stare us in the face," he wrote. "Nothing ahead to eat; an enemy behind and before us." Sibley, however, chose to push on, and on March 7, the Second Texas occupied Albuquerque, hoisting the Confederate flag on the main plaza, firing thirteen cannon in salute, and despite the destruction of the military supplies by the withdrawing Federals, confiscating "a Yankee store" of enough material to last them for approximately forty days.[15]

From there, Sibley sent Pyron's battalion on to Santa Fe. Lieutenant Colonel Scurry, with the Fourth and a battalion of William Steele's regiment, was pushed forward in the direction of Galisteo, whereas Green, with his regiment, was held at Albuquerque to check any movement up from Fort Craig. Still, Sibley remained ignorant of the Federals' location, numbers, and purposes. "We have heard various reports of their intentions," wrote Peticolas. Some rumors had the enemy recruiting their army with a view to attacking the Confederates, while others had Canby leaving Craig with eight hundred men and making for Fort Union to make another stand. Yet another was that three thousand Colorado volunteers—"Pikes Peakers," as the Rebels called them—were lying in the path. To Judge Baird's "certain knowledge" 8000 regulars and 1,300 Colorado volunteers were at Fort Craig. "We don't know what they're doing," Peticolas admitted.[16]

In fact, Canby was still at Fort Craig with his regulars, Colorado volunteers, and Kit Carson's New Mexico regiment, and the First Colorado Volunteers were languishing in a camp of instruction at Denver. There, on March 1, they received word of the defeat at Valverde and the rumor that Fort Craig had fallen. "Marching orders were immediately published, and gave universal joy." After a day and a half of what Captain Ovando J. Hollister described as "convulsive effort" the regiment was on the march to Fort Union through "a most distressing snow-storm." Knowing that the Texans had cut communication between Canby and Santa Fe and Fort Union, that Santa Fe was taken, and Fort Union "would share its fate and all the its vast military stores would fall into the hands of the enemy, unless we reached there in time to prevent their doing it," the volunteers were asked if they were "willing to endure the fatigues of forced marches in order to save the honor and prosperity of the Republic." The "Colorados," according to Hollister, responded with a unanimous "yes we will go," and from the Red River to Fort Union the volunteers marched as much as sixty miles in a day, subsisting on hard tack, "with the additional luxury of a canteen of water when it could be obtained."[17]

The regiment's lieutenant colonel, Samuel F. Tappan, concluded to "hurry forward as fast as possible," and by March 4, the troops, having sent back all baggage but a change of shirts and pair of blankets for each man, had reached Bent's Old Fort on the Santa Fe Trail. Crossing the Arkansas River on March 5, they marched seventy-five miles "with little water and less timber" to the Purgatoire, which they struck on the seventh at the base of the Raton Mountains. Since the men had left Denver "in a comparative state of destitution," Hollister admitted, "they were obliged to pick up such little conveniences as teams and wagons along the way." If such extralegal requisitions gave offense, he rather disingenuously pleaded, "it should be attributed to the pressure of circumstances."[18]

On the Purgatoire the regiment's colonel, John P. Slough, arrived, relieving Lieutenant Colonel Tappan. "He has a noble appearance," said Hollister, "but the men seem to lack confidence in him." Principally, complained Hollister, his "aristocratic style savors more of the eastern society than of the free-and-easy border, to which he should have become acclimated but that is bred in the bone." Also, although Slough had served as the regiment's colonel for six months, he had never addressed them, and even on the eve of their first campaign "could not see that a few words were indispensable to a good understanding." And, worse,

Samuel F. Tappan

Tappan was born on June 29, 1831, at Manchester, Massachusetts, into a prominent New England family. In August 1854, as part of the New England Emigrant Aid Company, he joined a group of twenty-nine Abolitionists who founded Lawrence, Kansas, in an attempt to bring Kansas into the Union as a Free State. As a correspondent for Horace Greeley's New York *Tribune*, he reported on the growing conflict in "Bleeding Kansas" and was active in the Underground Railroad, the smuggling of arms to so-called *Jayhawker paramilitary units*, as well as territorial politics, serving in 1857 as Speaker of the Topeka House of Representatives.

In 1860, Tappan moved to the Colorado gold fields where he reported for the Denver *Daily Herald*, speculated in real estate, and dabbled in mining. With the outbreak of the Civil War, territorial governor William C. Gilpin authorized Tappan to help raise the First Colorado Volunteer regiment, of which he was commissioned lieutenant colonel under Colonel John P. Slough. In temporary command of the regiment, in March 1862, Tappan reinforced Fort Union, then threatened by Brigadier General Henry Hopkins Sibley's Confederate Army of New Mexico and saw action in the battles of Pigeon's Ranch and Glorieta Pass. When Slough resigned as colonel a few days after the battle at Glorieta, Tappan became the regiment's acting colonel but relinquished the command in favor of its major, John M. Chivington. After an act of perceived insubordination in 1863, however, Chivington relegated Tappan to the command of Fort Garland in southern Colorado. Tappan was appointed to head the military commission that investigated Chivington's 1864 attack on Chief Black Kettle's band of peaceful Cheyennes. The investigation excoriated Chivington for his role in the so-called Sand Creek Massacre, but he received no official punishment.

At the end of the war Tappan was mustered out of the army with a brevet promotion to the rank of colonel. Much of his postwar career centered on his efforts to gain equal civil rights for American Indians. In July 1867, for example, President Andrew Johnson appointed him as a member of the commission that negotiated the Medicine Lodge Treaty, and he served on the committee that at last released the Apaches and Navajos from the notorious Bosque Redondo reservation. Tappan died in Washington on January 6, 1913, and is buried in the Arlington National Cemetery.

John P. Slough

Slough was born on February 1, 1829, in Cincinnati, Ohio, where he was a practicing attorney and served in the state's general assembly until he was expelled for striking a fellow representative. He then moved to Denver, Colorado Territory, in 1860 and in August 1861, was commissioned colonel of the First Colorado Volunteers. At Fort Union, although subordinate to Colonel Edward R. S. Canby, commander of the Department of New Mexico, he assumed command of the Union forces in the northern part of the territory, then facing the invasion of Brigadier General Henry Hopkins Sibley's brigade of Texas cavalry.

Slough intercepted and engaged the vanguard of the Confederate force at Glorieta Pass while Major John M. Chivington, in a daring flank march, destroyed its supply train. Despite the decisive victory at Glorieta, Slough resigned his command and traveled to Washington, D.C., where he was given a brigade stationed at Harpers Ferry in the Shenandoah Valley. Although he saw little action, he was promoted to brigadier general of volunteers on August 25, 1862, and was appointed commander of the Military District of Alexandria.

At the war's end, President Andrew Johnson appointed Slough as chief justice of the Supreme Court of New Mexico. His attempts to end the corruption that was endemic in territorial institutions, including the system peonage, proved unpopular, however, and on December 16, 1867, he was shot in Santa Fe by William Logan Rynerson, a member of the Territorial Legislative Council, and died on the following day.

while the men endured a forced march and the mules "began to drop and die in harness, from overwork and underfeed," Slough rode in a coach, further failing to endear himself to his men.[19]

Cresting the Rocky Mountains at noon on March 9, the regiment could "imagine, rather than see, the promised land were battles were to be fought and glory achieved." Debouching from Raton Pass, Hollister found a scene "wild and picturesque; too sunshiny and interesting for my ideas of New Mexico," but there the regiment received "some jumbled intelligence" regarding the Confederate threat to Fort Union, "upon which we added

Gabriel R. Paul

Paul was born in St. Louis, Missouri, on March 22, 1813, and graduated from the U.S. Military Academy, ranking eighteenth of the thirty-six cadets in the class of 1834. Assigned to the Seventh U.S. Infantry, he served in the Seminole Wars and the Mexican War, sustaining a wound at Cerro Gordo and returning to duty before the capture Mexico City; he received a brevet to major for his role in the storming of Chapultepec.

Paul began the Civil War as major of the Eighth U.S. Infantry and in December 1861, was appointed colonel of the Fourth New Mexico Infantry at Fort Union. Captain Ovando J. Hollister characterized him as "a sterling officer—one of the few never cursed by the soldiers."

At the end of the New Mexico campaign he was transferred to the Army of the Potomac as a brigadier general lead a brigade in Major General John F. Reynolds's I Corps at Chancellorsville and Gettysburg. In the latter battle he was seriously wounded, leaving him totally blind. He was nevertheless kept on the army rolls until February 1865, when he was retired from the service. Paul died in Washington, D.C., on May 5, 1886, and was buried in Arlington National Cemetery.

wings to our speed" and marched the final eighty miles to its destination. At last, on March 11, the Colorado volunteers arrived at Fort Union, "a simple field-work of moderate size, with bastioned corners surrounded by dirt parapet and ditch, with a slight abattis at exposed points." Bomb-proof quarters formed part of the works, and although Hollister judged the armament to be poor—consisting mostly of howitzers—he deemed the ammunition supply "sufficient for any emergency."[20]

They were greeted by Henry Connelly, New Mexico's governor-in-exile, and the post's commandant, Colonel Gabriel R. Paul of the Fourth New Mexico Volunteers, who Hollister characterized as "a sterling officer—one of the few never cursed by the soldiers." Immediately upon arriving, Slough relieved Paul of the command of the Northern District of New Mexico, which, with the advent of the Colorado regiment, consisted of 1,342 officers and men and 2 four-gun batteries, including Captain William Henry Lewis's company of the Fifth U.S. Infantry, and "such New Mexico volunteers as he found at Fort Union." With these, Slough prepared to either defend the route to the north or to unite with Canby's force, which he thought to be on the march from Fort Craig.[21]

Although the Colorado men groused about their reception at Fort Union, the regulars there, "probably 400," Hollister estimated, were glad of their arrival. "It was an undisguised fact that the Texans were having it their own way in the territory," but little was known for certain about the location or numbers of Sibley's command. "Madame Rumor has kindly furnished the news" that it was in Santa Fe, and "recruits are rapidly swelling his ranks. His number is variously estimated at from 25 to 3500."[22]

Based on such limited intelligence, Slough marched out of Fort Union on March 22, reaching Bernal Springs on the twenty-sixth. There, he dispatched Major John M. Chivington, a Methodist minister in civilian life and former presiding elder of the new Rocky Mountain District, with a detachment of 200 cavalry and 180 infantry in advance of the main column. "I think it was the intention to make a sudden dash on Santa Fe with this force," Hollister speculated, "and if possible take it by surprise." Having received information that some six hundred Texans from Santa Fe were at Pigeon's Ranch, five miles ahead, however, Chivington's detachment halted for the night at Martin Kozlowski's ranch.[23]

The equally ill-informed Confederates, meanwhile, had established headquarters at Albuquerque, with their main force encamped twenty miles to the east. "I think we will move in a few days" for Santa Fe, Sergeant Starr wrote on March 16. "According to the most reliable information we can get, the regulars at Fort Craig, the Mexicans having deserted, are leaving it in small parties with the intention of passing around us and concentrating at Fort Union." The Texans expected to intercept them before they made the junction, however, "which will put us in possession of the whole territory."[24]

John M. Chivington

Chivington was born on January 27, 1821, in Lebanon, Ohio, and was ordained as a minister in the Methodist church in 1844. After ten years of service to the Payson Circuit in the Illinois Conference, he became a missionary to the Wyandot Indians in Kansas in 1853, but left the territory due to his outspoken abolitionist views. The Methodist Church transferred Chivington to a parish in Omaha, Nebraska, which he left after only one year, due, apparently to his lack of suitability for the position. In May 1860, Chivington moved to Denver where he was elected as presiding elder of the Rocky Mountain District, serving until 1862 when he was not reappointed.

When the Civil War broke out, Colorado territorial governor William Gilpin offered him a commission as a chaplain, but Chivington refused it, preferring, instead, a line commission. He was therefore appointed as major of the First Colorado Volunteers under Colonel John P. Slough. On March 28, 1862, Slough sent Chivington and his detachment on a circling movement, with orders to strike the Confederate rear while Slough's main force engaged its front at Glorieta Pass, New Mexico. Chivington's command found the Rebel supply train largely undefended at Johnson's Ranch. He proceeded to burn the supply wagons and, according to a captured Confederate chaplain, threatened to kill the prisoners whom he took at Johnson's Ranch. Although the Confederates won the battle of Glorieta Pass, they lacked food and ammunition to sustain their advance and were forced to retreat to El Paso.

In April 1862, Chivington was appointed colonel of the newly organized Third Colorado Cavalry. With this undisciplined volunteer regiment, he attacked

As an advanced guard, on March 18, Sibley dispatched a battalion of four companies of the Fifth Texas under Major John S. Shropshire to meet Slough's advancing column in the mountains east of Santa Fe, where the constricted nature of the ground along the Santa Fe Trail would, to some degree, neutralize the Federals' numerical advantage. On the twenty-fifth, the Federal vanguard captured four Rebel pickets who, taking the Colorado troops for their own men, "rode into their midst before discovering their mistake." These prisoners confirmed the presence of a Confederate force, and the following morning Chivington moved on toward Santa Fe, thinking it likely that he "would meet a force of Texans during the day."[25]

the peaceful village of Cheyenne chief Black Kettle, located on Sand Creek in southeast Colorado Territory, on November 29, 1864, massacring and mutilating the bodies of between 150 and 200 Indians, nearly all of whom were women and children. Chivington's forces lost fifteen killed and more than fifty wounded, mostly due to friendly fire.

"Damn any man who sympathizes with Indians!" Chivington was quoted as saying. "I have come to kill Indians, and believe it is right and honorable to use any means under God's heaven to kill Indians. . . . Kill and scalp all, big and little; nits make lice."

The Joint Committee on the Conduct of the War condemned Chivington's actions in the strongest possible terms, stating that it could "hardly find fitting terms to describe his conduct. Wearing the uniform of the United States, which should be the emblem of justice and humanity; holding the important position of commander of a military district, and therefore having the honor of the government to that extent in his keeping, he deliberately planned and executed a foul and dastardly massacre which would have disgraced the verist [sic] savage among those who were the victims of his cruelty," but no criminal charges were brought against him. His political aspirations, however, were effectively ended.

Chivington resigned from the service in February 1865 and returned to Nebraska. There he became an unsuccessful freight hauler. He also seduced and then married his recently deceased son's widow, but in October 1871, she obtained a decree of divorce for non-support. After living briefly in California, Chivington farmed in Ohio, edited a local newspaper, and in 1883, ran unsuccessfully for a seat in the Ohio legislature. He then returned to Denver where he worked as a deputy sheriff until shortly before his death from cancer on October 4, 1894.

"We traveled all night," wrote Hollister, "rested at Kozlowski's, started again next morning and reached Pigeon's Ranche about noon" of the twenty-sixth. Just past Pigeon's Ranch, the Union pickets raced back to the column shouting, "We've got them corralled this time," "Give them hell boys," and "Hurrah for the Pike's Peakers." Some 250 Confederates—Pyron's battalion of the Second Texas and two howitzers—were halted at Johnson's Ranch in Apache Canyon, about fifteen miles southeast of Santa Fe on the road to Fort Union. Shropshire's battalion was within supporting distance, but not yet united with the main body. Chivington's men advanced up the canyon at "double-quick, march" to within three

John S. Shropshire

Shropshire was born on April 23, 1833, in Bourbon County, Kentucky, but he moved to Texas in 1854, settling in Columbus, Colorado County, where he practiced law. By 1860, Shropshire operated a 750-acre plantation, owned sixty-one slaves, and had more than $50,000 in personal estate. Despite his pro-Union views, Shropshire was commissioned as the major in the Fifth Texas Cavalry. On March 28, 1862, Shropshire was killed in action at the battle of Glorieta, but not until 1990 was his body identified and returned to his birthplace in Kentucky where it was reburied alongside his parents.

hundred yards of the Texans, who were unlimbering their two guns when the Federals came in sight.[26]

Chivington's men rushed into Apache Canyon, but came face to face with Pyron's two field pieces, less than two hundred yards distant, supported by a company of Texans "displaying a saucy little red flag" emblazoned with the Lone Star. The leading Union company "parted either way and filed to the rear in confusion" as the Rebel artillery opened fire, giving warning to Shropshire's battalion, which rode at once to the sound of the guns. The remaining Federals "instinctively crowded to the left to get out of range. All was confusion," Hollister admitted. Chivington, "of commanding presence, dressed in full regimentals," rallied his men, however, and the two Confederate guns "found their position in the road untenable and retired rapidly" a mile or so down the road westward toward Apache Canyon to redeploy under the protection of their infantry. Shropshire had by this time arrived to reinforce Pyron, and sent two companies deployed as skirmishers into the cliffs overlooking the field on each of Pyron's flanks.

The Federals followed cautiously, and Chivington, "with a pistol in each hand and one or two under his arms," deployed his cavalry to the right and left to envelope the new Southern position and sent his dismounted men climbing up the canyon sides "with considerable agility" to deploy as skirmishers. The ground was unfavorable for mounted operations, however, and the Confederates had assumed a strong natural position. "To dislodge them," Hollister wrote, "it was necessary to walk into their affections without ceremony." The Federals were convinced that "the bluffs and road were alive with Texans," and the Rebel battery, well supported, was laying down a heavy fire. "Their grapeshot," Hollister later recalled, "was rattling thick and fast over our heads, accompanied by an incessant fire of musketry, which soon had a telling effect." But when Chivington gave the order to attack, the Union cavalry surged forward and the Confederate artillery once again fell back down the canyon while the infantry, sheltered in the rocks on either side of the canyon, met the charge with "a redoubled shower of lead."[27]

The Union horsemen continued their sweep down the canyon in pursuit of the illusive artillery, but, lamented Hollister, "it was too fleet footed for us," and, armed with only revolvers, they were no match for the Rebels on the hillsides. "So the horsemen wheeled about and charged back up the road they had just charged down, this time aiding the Union infantry, which had just arrived on the field "like a parcel of wild Indians," in claiming some forty or fifty prisoners.[28]

When darkness fell, the Confederates withdrew to their supply train and established camp at Cañoncito or Johnson's Ranch, near the western entrance to Apache Canyon, and the Federals fell back to Pigeon's Ranch, there being no water in the canyon. "Thus ended our first battle," wrote Hollister. "We had driven them from their position under every disadvantage; killed and disabled fifty at least, and captured one-quarter of their entire number." Pyron's official report of the battle has never been located, so exact numbers cannot be determined, but Peticolas reported only two killed and three wounded, but seventy-one men taken prisoner. Chivington reported his loss to be five killed, fourteen wounded, and three missing. "How we escaped so cheaply," wrote Hollister, "God only knows, for we rode 500 yards through a perfect hail storm of bullets. Many men were lying behind rocks, almost near enough to knock us off our horses, taking dead rests and firing as we passed." Both sides claimed the victory in the battle of Apache Canyon. "If we had had two

William R. Scurry

Scurry of the Fourth Texas, wrote A. B. Peticolas, was "the best officer, most polished gentleman, most sociable gentleman, and the most popular colonel in the whole outfit." Scurry was born in Gallatin, Tennessee, on February 10, 1821, and arrived in Texas on June 20, 1839. There he was licensed to practice law and appointed district attorney of the fifth judicial district in 1841. Adolphus Sterne wrote in his diary that it was as "bad appointment. I respect the young man but will not do for that very, very, very responsible office." Scurry became aide-de-camp to Thomas Jefferson Rusk in 1842 and represented Red River County in the Ninth Congress of the Republic of Texas in 1844 and 1845. As a member of the House of Representatives in 1845, Scurry was energetic and effective in his support of the annexation of Texas to the United States. During the Mexican War he enlisted as a private in Colonel George T. Wood's Second Regiment, Texas Mounted Volunteers, and was promoted to major on July 4, 1846. After the war he practiced law in Clinton and until 1854 was the owner and editor, with Joseph Wade Hampton, of the Austin *State Gazette*. In 1856, Scurry was a delegate from Victoria County to the state Democratic nominating convention in Austin.

After representing Victoria, DeWitt, Jackson, and Calhoun counties in the Secession Convention, Scurry entered Confederate service in July 1861 as the lieutenant colonel of the Fourth Texas Mounted Rifles and greatly distinguished himself during the Confederate invasion of New Mexico, commanding the Confederate forces at the battle of Glorieta. He was promoted to colonel on March 28, 1862 and to brigadier general on September 12, 1862, and played a vital role in the Confederate recapture of Galveston on January 1, 1863. Scurry commanded the Third Brigade at the battles of Mansfield and Pleasant Hill in April 1864 and was immediately transferred with his command to Arkansas to help to repel the wing of the Federal army commanded by Frederick Steele, then marching toward Shreveport. Scurry was wounded at the battle of Jenkins Ferry on April 30, 1864, but he refused to be carried to the rear. A Federal attack overran the place where he lay, and for two hours his wound was unattended. When his brigade regained the field he asked, "Have we whipped them?" On being told that the battle was won, Scurry replied, "Now take me to a house where I can be made comfortable and die easy." He died of his wounds later that day.

hours more daylight," Hollister believed, "our victory would have been still more decisive. Darkness favored their escape." The hard day's fight was, in fact, no more than an indecisive skirmish.[29]

That evening, Chivington sent a message to Slough, stating that he had met and defeated the enemy, and the main body of the Federals was soon on the march to join him at Pigeon's Ranch. At the same time, Pyron, the senior Confederate officer on the field, sent for reinforcements. "He had been attacked by a large body of Pike's Peak men during the day," he informed Scurry, but "had gotten the best of the engagement and had fallen back to water," which he would hold until Scurry, sixteen miles away at Galisteo, came up to him. Scurry arrived at 3:00 on the morning of March 27 and assumed command. Colonel Green's regiment was still in Albuquerque with Sibley, and so too far away to come to the support of its comrades.[30]

At first light, Scurry, a lawyer and politician in civilian life, but a veteran of the Mexican War, deployed his forces to meet the expected Federal attack. "Finding a very strong natural position," wrote Peticolas, "we halted in line and began to increase the elevation of the bank behind which we were to fight. In our front the road passed through a narrow opening between the mountains. Behind us was a considerable hill bristling with our cannon, and on the sides of the mountains were placed our sharpshooters." Unfortunately for the Texans, however, "they did not come to attack, and we laid here all day awaiting them." "The enemy had made a good retreat," wrote Lieutenant Giesecke, "and did not try a second attack."[31]

After remaining all day in a defensive posture, Scurry determined to take the offensive. "We had been told by Colonel Scurry that if the enemy did not come to us that we would go to them," Peticolas recalled, so on the morning March 28, the Texans started down the Santa Fe Trail for the Federal camp at Pigeon Ranch, eight miles below. Apache Canyon was narrow and the slopes abrupt, scattered with masses of rock, and in the valley was a dense pine forest "where you cannot see a man at twenty steps unless he is moving," Peticolas recalled.[32]

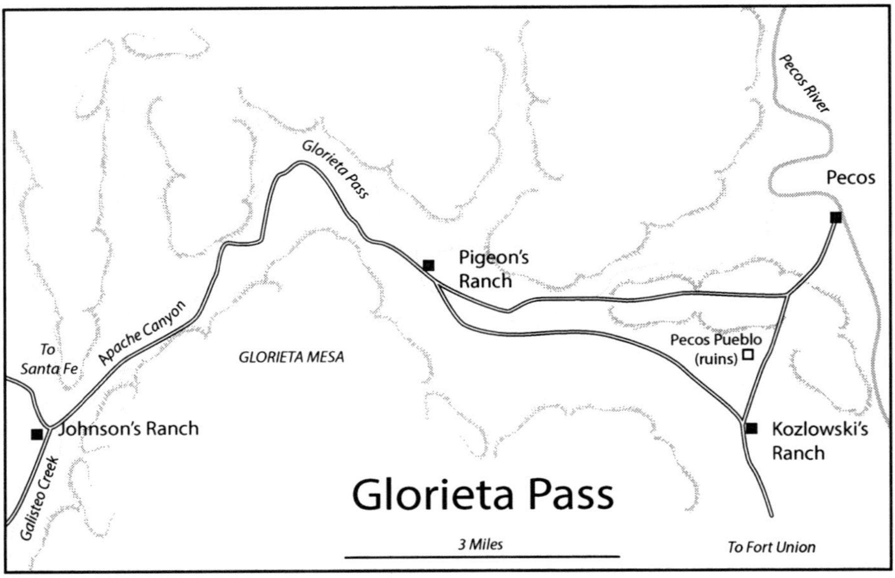

Leaving a small guard of noncombatants with his wagons, Scurry advanced with about six hundred men—nine companies of the First regiment, four each of the Second and Third, and Pyron's battalion, supported by two 6-pounder field guns and a 12-pounder field howitzer—to meet the Federals. "We left our wagons and went on foot to look up the enemy," said Giesecke. "We found them, 1400 men strong, in Glorieta Pass, six miles from our camp." By this time, however, Slough, with what Scurry characterized as "Pike's Peak miners and regulars, the flower of the United States army," had arrived from Vernal Spring to rejoin Chivington's detachment to meet the Confederate advance.[33]

As Scurry was marching toward Pigeon's Ranch, Slough, with the infantry companies of the First Colorado, two companies of regular cavalry, and two batteries—about six hundred men, in all—was moving down Glorieta Canyon, "not doubting but that every inch of ground would be stubbornly contested by the Rangers," wrote Hollister. "We knew nothing certainly of their force, either as to strength, disposition or intentions," and were taken almost entirely by surprise at Pigeon's Ranch when their pickets reported that the Texans were advancing in force, less than half a mile up the trail. At about 10:00 o'clock in the morning the opposing forces collided, many of the Federals becoming aware of the proximity of the Texans only "when their artillery commenced cutting the treetops over our heads."[34]

According to one Union soldier, "This was a terrible place for an engagement—a deep gorge, with a narrow wagon-track running along the bottom, the ground rising precipitously on each side, with huge bowlders and clumps of stunted cedars interspersed." The nature of the ground, rough, hilly, rocky, and timbered, rendered mounted cavalry almost useless. "The regular cavalry was of no account at all, for whenever the Texans came in sight they would mount and fall back out of range," Hollister claimed.[35]

When Scurry's and Slough's forces made initial contact, the Confederates dismounted and deployed in line of battle while the four Rebel guns unlimbered on a slight elevation to the rear and opened fire. As the Confederate infantry arrived, it, too, was thrown into line athwart the canyon. Slough, as well, dismounted his cavalry and positioned it under shelter of a small hill, brought up his two batteries—six 12-pounder howitzers and two 6-pounder "shot-guns"—and deployed his infantry behind an adobe wall, which ran nearly the width of the canyon, and in the rocks of the canyon sides.[36]

All day, from ten in the morning until five in the afternoon, the Texans launched a series of attacks against this formidable Union line in what Scurry characterized as "the hardest contested fight it had ever been my lot to witness." Frontal attacks proved unavailing, and Union fire on the Rebel battery "became so hot that the artillerymen could not stand it," and the gunners limbered up and departed, with the battery commander severely wounded. Major Shropshire was killed and his senior company commander, Captain Shannon, was captured.[37]

The only Federal tactical offensive of the engagement came when one company of the "Colorados," taking advantage of a gulch that ran toward the Confederate line, attempted to capture the Rebel battery. According to Hollister, if this attack had been supported, the Confederates "never would have taken their artillery from the field," but "these brave boys paid dearly for their temerity." Upon discovering the presence of the concealed company, the Confederates "dashed down upon them with a yell and plunging into the gully came to a hand-to-hand conflict with them," wrote Peticolas. Scurry's counterattack fell on the isolated company with knives and pistols. In the gulch, according to Scurry, "a most desperate and deadly hand-to-hand conflict ensued," and, having lost one-half of their men, the Federals broke off the action and retired to their original line "in the wildest disorder and confusion."[38]

Although Hollister said that "many of the boys thought our Sharps inspired more terror, even at five hundred yards' distance than the batteries opposite," the big guns so dominated the bottom of the canyon and the Santa Fe Trail that what he characterized as "the hard breast to breast fighting" was done on the flanks, in the boulders on the canyon sides. Twice the Texans were able to turn the Union line, and twice the Federals fell back to strong positions farther down the canyon. "About noon," said Hollister, "we were forced to retire our whole line half a mile, as they had discovered our weakness and were endeavoring to surround us."[39]

"If the Texans had known how weak we were doubtless they would have ruined us," Hollister opined, "but the lesson of the day before made them cautious. They would creep along up from tree to tree, and from rock to rock." Peticolas agreed that "we all fought in the same way, advancing steadily from tree to tree and shooting at every enemy that showed himself." Such cautious tactics seem to have been entirely justified, for when the Federals rallied for a second time, at a ledge of rocks in the rear, there, wrote Scurry, "they made their final and most desperate stand." Seeking to capitalize on the Confederate advantage, Scurry launched a frontal assault, "encouraged and shouted on by as brave officers as live," but the Federal gunners waited until they came within fifty yards before opening on them, playing "the liveliest Yankee Doodle ever heard." At the point, the charging Texans "all began to find some safe place behind the corrals and houses and trees" Peticolas admitted.[40]

"The time gained by this repulse enabled us to extricate ourselves from our perilous position, move back, and take a new stand." There the Federals held their ground until their artillery and wagon train was withdrawn to the camp. Only then, with a third general assault, did the Confederates succeed in driving their infantry from the field. According to Scurry, the remaining Federals broke ranks and fled, setting fire to two of their wagons. The Confederates pursued the defeated enemy until forced by exhaustion to halt, but this was to be the high water mark of the Confederate campaign.[41]

"We were obliged to give ground from the commencement," Hollister conceded, "yet considering the disparity of our forces (by their own admission they had 1800) we were well satisfied." Under the cover of darkness, the Federals retired to Kozlowski Ranch, and Scurry claimed the field and the victory, but the day had, in fact, been disastrous for the Confederates.[42]

In the masterstroke of the campaign, while the larger battle was going on at Pigeon's Ranch, Chivington's column was crossing the heavily wooded Glorieta Mesa, which bordered the Santa Fe Trail on the south and ended directly above the Confederate camp at Cañoncito. Descending the mesa, it fell on the Confederate wagon guard—some two hundred sick and disabled men—capturing sixteen of their number and driving the rest toward Santa Fe. The raiders then destroyed sixty wagons with the Confederates' reserve ammunition, baggage, food, forage, and medicines, and spiked one 6-pounder gun. As Pettis observed, "this loss was the most serious that the enemy had met with in the whole of their campaign," as all their supplies—of which they were already short—were lost. Scurry believed that, having destroyed their supply train, Chivington would have attacked the Confederate rear had he not learned from a party of liberated Federal prisoners that Slough had been defeated at Pigeon's Ranch and was in retreat. He, therefore, chose to return to Kozlowski's, "every man taking his own course."[43]

"Thus ended the battle of Glorieta Valley, in which we gained a complete victory but at the expense of every comfort," wrote Peticolas.

Henry W. Raguet

Raguet was born in Cincinnati, Ohio, on June 29, 1824, but in 1834 his family resettled in the area of Nacogdoches, Texas. In 1852 he assumed control of the family's highly profitable mercantile business. When the Civil War began, Raguet enlisted as a private in Tom Green's Fourth Texas Mounted Rifles, but quickly moved up the ranks from lieutenant to captain and, on August 23, 1861, to major. Raguet was wounded in the leg at the battle of Valverde but recovered in time to take part in the battle of Glorieta in which he was mortally wounded. He is buried in the Odd Fellows Cemetery at Santa Fe, New Mexico.

The Confederates reported their losses at the battle of Glorieta at thirty-six killed, sixty wounded, and sixteen captured. "That of the enemy greatly exceeded this number," Scurry believed, but Slough estimated the Federal loss at forty-four killed, sixty-four wounded, and thirty missing. Among the Texan dead were the popular Shropshire and Raguet. An exchange of prisoners was precluded by the Federals' refusal to consent to "an even exchange between Mexicans and whites."[44]

Much more important to the future of the campaign than the casualties was the loss of the Confederate supply train. This irreparable blow compelled the Texans to evacuate the territory. Had the Federals known the extent of the injury that Chivington's audacious raid had inflicted, they might have taken Santa Fe by the next day. As it was, the Confederates remained on the field "without food, near a fire, but froze no little," through March 29, burying their dead and tending to their wounded. "We got some dried buffalo beef and at a ranch a little back where the Ab[olitionist]s had it stored and we lined our haversacks pretty bountifully with it," Peticolas reported.[45]

But beyond that, "what was going to become of us we hardly knew," wrote Lieutenant Giesecke, "as it was said that the Yankees had taken charge and were guarding the pass at our old camp at Apache Canyon, cutting off our way to Santa Fe almost entirely." Scurry's men were too weak to attack the Federals in a strong position, but by evening they determined "to gain Santa Fe by attacking the pass at the risk of our lives." They marched toward Apache Canyon just at dark, but found no enemy blocking their path. Late in the evening of the twenty-ninth, as Peticolas recalled, Scurry gave the order "to get our guns to march," and at about 10:00 o'clock that night, the veterans of Glorieta started for Santa Fe, twenty-two miles distant, arriving just at daybreak. "The hunger and fatigue of our men was great," recorded Giesecke with grim understatement.[46]

Slough, "having accomplished all that was desired," returned to Fort Union, arriving at sundown on April 2. "We had been gone eleven days—traveled seventy-five miles, fought in two battles," wrote Hollister, and "were glad of a chance to rest." Although he admitted that the Colorado volunteers were "half glad to escape the renewal of yesterday," they were also revolted at "backing out before we were well whipped." The, to him, "inexplicable" order to retreat, he inferred, came from Colonel Canby, "and Canby was the commanding officer." Colonel Slough, who Hollister characterized as "a thorough fighting-man," shortly thereafter resigned his commission, indicating to Hollister that he was dissatisfied with the order to retreat, but was compelled to obey.[47]

Before leaving Glorieta Canyon, Scurry issued a general order complementing his soldiers for having "added another victory to the long list of triumphs won by the Confederate armies"—one which would entitle them to "stand by the side of those who fought and conquered on the red field of San Jacinto." But although Scurry exhorted his men to "go on as you have commenced, and it will not be long until not a single soldier of the United States will be left on the soil of New Mexico," it was clear that the Rebel tide had broken on the rock of Chivington's raid and that the Army of New Mexico could not long hold the conquests it had made. Scurry's boast that "the Territory, relieved of the burdens recently imposed upon it by its late oppressors, will once more, throughout its beautiful valleys, "blossom as the rose," beneath the plastic hand of peaceful industry," rang with false hope.[48]

6

"IT SEEMED IMPOSSIBLE FOR MEN TO HAVE MADE THEIR WAY.": THE RETREAT

Lieutenant Colonel William R. Scurry's "Advanced Division" returned to Santa Fe almost destitute; "the quartermasters and commissary department are hard at work preparing to supply our wants in the clothing and blanket line." The men also began to equip themselves. Private William H. Smith boasted that the Texans "captured about $20,000.00 worth of groceries such as salt, coffee, sugar, molasses, whiskey etc." Although Alfred B. Peticolas reported that $30,000 worth of Federal property had been confiscated and that local citizens were immensely kind, there was "very poor eating." With "no bacon or pork, and very little coffee," the men were "living on cornmeal."[1]

On April 1, the Federals began their campaign to remove the Confederates from New Mexico. Leaving Colonel Kit Carson with the First New Mexico to garrison Fort Craig, Colonel Edward R. S. Canby led 860 regulars and 350 volunteers with four pieces of artillery up the Rio Grande to confront Brigadier General Henry Hopkins Sibley. On the fifth, Colonel Gabriel R. Paul at Fort Union—once again, with Colonel

John P. Slough's resignation, in command of the Northern District of New Mexico—received Canby's orders to "pack up, and be ready to start in an hour." As Canby's column approached the Confederates from the south, Paul's twelve hundred regulars and Colorado volunteers were to "divert the enemy's attention, or assist in driving him out of the country." The Colorado volunteers, all mounted, started their march south on April 6. The weather, according to Captain Ovando J. Hollister, was "windy and disagreeable" and desertion rates were alarming.[2]

Learning of Scurry's precarious situation, Sibley, with Colonel Tom Green and the Second Texas and Teel's artillery, marched to his assistance, reaching Santa Fe on April 5, further taxing an already overstrained commissary. Sibley had left only two companies with three or four pieces of artillery—about two hundred men—to guard the supply depot at Albuquerque, and Canby was in position to easily overpower this feeble garrison and then join forces with Paul's column from Fort Union, thus giving him significant numerical superiority over the beleaguered Confederates. Albuquerque, in Hollister's estimation, was "the place for the Texans to meet us" if they wished to prevent the junction of the two Federal forces. Their failure to do so, he reasoned, revealed the Rebels' intention "to give up the occupation of the territory, or let it out at least."[3]

Had he then chosen to do so, Canby could have forced another battle with Sibley's ragged command at Santa Fe, with every expectation of decisive success. Ever cautious—and like Winfield Scott, George B. McClellan, Henry W. Halleck, and so many Union commanders in the early stages of the war, preferring to win by maneuver rather than by fighting the costly set piece battle—Canby instead chose to maneuver the Rebels out of Santa Fe by threatening their supply depot at Albuquerque, to meld his command Paul's in the Sandina Mountains east of that town, and then to harry the Confederates back down the Rio Grande and out of New Mexico. The Federal threat to Albuquerque forced Sibley to countermarch Green's regiment to the defense of the Rebel base on April 7, only two days after its arrival in Santa Fe.[4]

Canby reached Albuquerque on April 8, "marching up as if he was coming into the town without noticing our men at all," wrote Sergeant Frank Starr to his father, "but when he had come within cannon range, Colonel James Reily threw shot among them so well directed and with such effect that they hauled off a short distance, encamping a little more than a mile off." The companies of Captains William P. "Old Gotch" Hardeman and Bethel Coopwood repulsed Canby's half-hearted attempt on the town's defenses. Although McLeary insisted that Canby's army outnumbered Hardeman's force of 130 to 250 men "by at least four to one, perhaps as much as ten to one," the attempt on Albuquerque was almost exclusively an artillery duel. "Canby had his two 24-pounders up and threw two or three bombs into the town," wrote Peticolas, "but did no damage." Hardeman's 6-pounders were said to have killed two or three of the enemy and wounded one. For four days and nights Canby invested Albuquerque, shelling the town, but not wishing perhaps to have to feed and guard prisoners, the Federals did not come nearer than eight hundred yards to the Confederate line.[5]

The country was, after all, stripped of provisions, Canby's own troops were on short rations, and Albuquerque was one thousand miles from his base of supplies. The defenders, however, thought that Canby's threat was quite real, and during the siege "all was anxiety and impatience for the arrival of the reinforcements," Starr wrote. On April 10, as soon as the news reached him that Albuquerque was under attack, Sibley marched out of Santa Fe to the defense of his depot and, at around noon on April 12, Green's regiment arrived, "putting all in high spirits for the next day's encounter." That afternoon, Canby demonstrated against the town but failed to attack, and the Confederates "were obliged to act on the defensive and not bring on the battle as we usually did by attacking them. Our ammunition was too scarce to hazard a fight, so we held our position."[6]

That night, the remainder of the Texas brigade reached the beleaguered town, "perfectly worn out with our efforts," only to learn that Canby was no longer there. Under the cover of darkness, the Federals had slipped away, and on the following morning "nothing could be seen of the enemy." The defenders of Albuquerque reacted to news of Canby's withdrawal with great joy, feeling that they had driven the enemy away and won an important victory. Captain William Lee Alexander believed that the Texans "had the enemy so well thrashed that 1000 would not attack a town defended by 150." Hardeman's heroic defense, according to Private James H. McLeary, "saved the town and the commissary stores on which Sibley depended to feed his men," and Texas historian John Henry Brown went so far as to say that "this defense saved the army."[7]

In fact, however, Canby seems to have had no intention of capturing Albuquerque but wanted only to push Sibley down the Rio Grande. He achieved that end, first by maneuvering the Confederates out of Santa Fe and then slipping through Carnuel Canyon to San Antonio on the east side of Sandia Mountain where, on April 13, he united with Paul's column, giving him a combined command of slightly more than twenty-four hundred men. With the two Union forces united, Hollister predicted, the Rebels "must show a clean pair of heels and a decided progress Texas-ward or fight."[8]

"Our condition there was indeed a bad one," Sergeant Starr agreed. According to, him, there was not enough ammunition left for a full day's fight, and worse, Peticolas reported that "there is not ten days' rations for the brigade above Craig," absolutely necessitating a retreat to prevent the army from starving. The territory contained no subsistence except that stored at Fort Union and Fort Craig and that which was well hidden by the people. This they could not purchase, having no money except Confederate currency, which was valueless to local farmers and ranchers. Fort Union and Fort Craig could withstand any siege or assault that the Confederates might throw against them. Sibley's only option was to retreat to the Mesilla Valley where Colonel William Steele and the Third Texas could provide some supplies and reinforcements, if only Canby would allow him to do so.[9]

Not wishing to chance another pitched battle, Canby was, indeed, willing to allow Sibley to slip away unscathed if only he would do so, and the Texas column, like a rattlesnake, was willing to slither away but was yet able to strike if pressed. Realizing that his already tenuous hold on the upper Rio Grande was now untenable, Sibley ordered the evacuation of Albuquerque to commence on the morning of April 12, when Scurry, Steele, and Major Charles Pyron crossed to the west bank of the river on a ferry boat and went into camp three miles downstream near village of Atrisco. Green's Fifth Texas, which was still mounted, was ordered not to attempt to cross at the ferry because it was too slow a process, but rather to move down the east bank and cross at the first practicable ford. From there, the Texans, "with empty stomachs for a tramp of forty miles," headed south. For three days they continued downstream, the command divided "as if despising their antagonists or inviting attack."[10]

The first ford that Green came to south of Albuquerque was so deep and so full of quicksand that the regiment's broken down mules could not pull the wagons across. Green, therefore, pitched camp on the east side of the river in and around Governor Henry Connelly's residence and surrounding fields, immediately north of the village of Peralta and about three miles across the river from Sibley's main camp at Los Lunas, intending to cross at the hard bottomed ford there. Canby, taking advantage of the situation, turned quickly and marched thirty-six miles to Peralta to attack the isolated Fifth regiment before Green, believing that the Federals were still in the vicinity of Galisteo, was aware of his approach. The Texan officers, according to Hollister, "were carousing at a fandango" in the governor's mansion, while Canby positioned his infantry and battery of 24-pounder howitzers north of the Rebels' camp, with his cavalrymen and light battery to the east. "The sounds of the fandango carried into the morning hours," observed Lieutenant Joseph M. Bell, commanding the reconstituted Alexander McRae's Battery, mingled with the "hilarious shouts of some overexcited participant. All was merry as a feast within the dark outline of the town, just growing visible in the gloomy twilight of approaching day. There we lay in the restrained excitement of the situation."[11]

The Federal troops "expected to attack immediately, and impatiently awaited the order to advance." When the order failed to arrive, Hollister complained, "words failed to express the disgust of the volunteers." Major John M. Chivington volunteered to attack the village with his regiment alone, but the general, "either afraid of the result, or jealous of us, would not consent." Thus, Hollister maintained, Canby allowed yet another opportunity pass.[12]

With the dawning of April 15, both camps awoke to "the thrilling reveille from Sibley's bugles, which was followed up by the stirring strains of 'Dixie,'" performed by the brigade's brass band. Soon, however, cannon fire awakened the Confederates to their present danger, and to the disaster they had so narrowly avoided the previous night. Just north of the village, Federal cavalry snapped up one of the Rebels' remaining mountain howitzers and seven wagons loaded with supplies, "though nothing of any great value," Hollister admitted, mired in the deep sands and further immobilized by the weakness of the teams. Only then did Canby move to attack Green.[13]

Appraised by a galloper from Green's staff of the situation at Peralta, Sibley, Scurry, and Captain Trevanian T. Teel attempted to cross the icy river to reinforce their embattled comrades but found the ford blocked by Federal forces. Quickly recovering from their initial shock, however, Green's gunners charged their four howitzers with canister and placed them "so as to sweep every street and opening," and his dismounted cavalrymen assumed a strong defensive position. Although Green had only 550 men to defend the place, Peralta was a veritable fortress of thick adobe houses and walls, *acequias* that easily doubled as field-works, and groves of cottonwood trees, from behind which the defenders could inflict unacceptable damage on an attacker. Thus, the Rebel line was "as secure a defense as though built under the special direction of a skillful engineer," Peticolas maintained. Somewhat more colorfully, Hollister stated his opinion that "a better place for bushwacking was never seen."[14]

The Federals deployed in line of battle facing Peralta and were met by the fire of a howitzer in the steeple of the Catholic Church. On slightly higher ground and sheltered behind the acequia, the Confederate gunners had the Federals' range precisely, and Hollister admitted that "sitting a horse on a high bridge, watching this artillery practice," was "not *exactly* interesting, but disagreeable." Throughout the day the Federal cavalry "was here, there and everywhere; now preparing to charge, now on foot advancing as skirmishers; always about to do something, but never doing it." All believed that "at a given signal we were to assault and take the place by storm." Canby, however, believed the defenses at Peralta to be "the strongest (except Fort Union) in New Mexico," and so, once again, declined to give the order to attack.[15]

The rest of the so-called battle of Peralta was pure anticlimax. "A sharp rattling exchange of cannonading was occasionally kept up during the day," wrote Hollister, but the Union line came no nearer to the village. Neither, on the other hand, would the Confederates leave their fortifications. Hollister grumbled that Canby's men challenged Green's "to a fair opened battle. But it was of no use, they would neither be tempted or coaxed out." The entire action consisted in "the firing of a few shots with small arms and a few rounds of artillery from each side," wrote Peticolas, and when a dust storm blew into the area in the late afternoon, Green availed himself of its cover to cross his command to the other side of the river. "It was the most harmless battle on record," Hollister conceded. The only Rebel casualty was one man wounded by friendly fire. The Federal loss was approximately four killed and three wounded.[16]

The Texans would maintain that they had heroically held Peralta, as they had Albuquerque, against superior numbers, and the Federals' "voluntary retiring from it proves them irreparably lame *somewhere*." Canby, however, was happy enough to allow Green to cross the Rio Grande to join the rest of the Army of New Mexico on its long and arduous retreat to the south. The Federal commander, it seems, had no intention of throwing away men in a battle that he did not need to win; his only desire was to drive the Confederates out of the territory. Hollister correctly surmised that the retreating Confederates were "destitute of all kinds of stores necessary for the prosecution of the war. They are too far from their base of operations."[17]

With his failure at Valverde already haunting him, Canby was again damned by both his troops and by the Unionist element of the civilian population for his policy of allowing his crippled enemy to escape. "As it is always fashionable to abuse everything that looks like cowardice, the General was castigated unmercifully that night," Hollister observed. "With a superior, better-appointed force, we had fired a few artillery shots; had been drawn up in line of battle six hours, just beyond rifle range of the foe, and finally hauled off with the immense loss of two killed," he bitterly complained. Although Canby's force outnumbered Sibley's by two to one and presumably could have taken in the Texans at any time, the Federal commander followed cautiously, keeping to the east bank, and although within cannon range, choosing not impeded the Rebel retreat, considering it "more expedient," in George Pettis's opinion, "to allow them to retreat out of the wilderness . . . than to capture the entire party and be forced to subsist them."[18]

In the midst of lackadaisical the pursuit, the First Colorado got a new commander. On April 14, Lieutenant Colonel Samuel F. Tappan "generously waived his rank in favor of Major Chivington," who Canby appointed as colonel. Chivington, wrote Hollister, "had always been a favorite with officers and men," and in accepting the command announced that "his sole and only rule would be, to do his duty without fear, favor or affection, and that when the time for action would arrive he would venture to predict that he would be found ready at his post in the hour of danger."[19]

On the morning of the sixteenth, the reunited Sibley Brigade resumed its march down the river. The disgusted Hollister, balked of what he was sure would have been the final blow of the New Mexico campaign, sarcastically observed that "though well-assured the enemy was on the other side of the river, and some distance below," Canby "maneuvered around Peralta something like a dog round a rattle snake," before entering the deserted town. Then, "having waited long enough to avoid all risk of collision with the Texas rear-guard," followed the refugee Confederates.[20]

The Rebels, too, wondered at Canby's restraint. Although "that confounded cavalry" shadowed them by day, occasionally skirmishing with the pickets, "the enemy would never take up the gauntlet" to cross the river for a showdown battle. All day on April 17, Peticolas wrote, the brigade expected an attack but did not have its expectations realized, and "it began to puzzle me to know what they were up to." The spectacle of "two hostile armies marching side by side down on opposite sides of the same river and in full view of each other" was, to him, entirely novel, and he could only conclude that the Federals were either "afraid of us and did not care to hazard crossing the river" or intended "to beat us to Craig, throw heavy reinforcements into the fort enough to hold it, and then close in behind us and compel us to surrender." Still confident of the Texans' ability to defeat Canby in open battle, Peticolas asserted that "we have whipped some of them twice," and was sure that "we can clean them up again" and break through to fresh supplies at Mesilla. That bravado began to fade when the Rebels realized that Canby's force, which they believed to have been heavily reinforced by troops marching from Kansas by way of Fort Union, now numbered six thousand on their rear, two thousand on their flank, and six hundred in Fort Craig in front. "Now," wrote Peticolas, "our position begins to be quite critical, and the object of the enemy begins to be apparent." Canby, he was sure, intended to surround the Sibley Brigade and compel it to surrender.[21]

The two armies trekked on across terrain that Hollister considered "perfectly worthless—nothing but drifting sand," always with the Confederates two or three hours ahead. "They certainly have nothing to fear from us so long as they keep going, be it ever so slow." That evening, both went into camp on opposite sides of the river between Sabinal and La Joya, but on the following morning the Confederates seemed to have disappeared. Canby's scouts reported that the enemy, emulating George Washington's ploy during the Princeton campaign of 1776, had left their camp fires burning and abandoned their camp during the night.[22]

Sibley later made the claim that he intended, after leaving Albuquerque, to outmarch Canby and attack Fort Craig before relief could arrive, but after the skirmish at Peralta, he continued slowly down the right bank of the Rio Grande, occasionally skirmishing with New Mexican militia, with Canby's forces following on the opposite side, in sight of one another. Although speed was essential to the success of Sibley's plan, his men traveled only ten or twelve miles a day. "They did not exhibit any unseemly haste," said Hollister. "The road is very heavy with sand," Peticolas recorded in his journal, "and our wagons cannot travel very fast."[23]

Too weak to attack Fort Craig, and with Canby closely shadowing him, Sibley was compelled to bypass the Federal stronghold going down the river, as he had coming up. "It was very plain to us that Canby could reach Fort Craig before we could," Sargent Starr observed. The pursuing Federals greatly outnumbered the Confederates, but "could not be made to attack us in our position, and our ammunition was too scarce for a general engagement." To continue toward Fort Craig, to return up river, or to stay where they were "would have been ruin to us."[24]

Seemingly trapped, Sibley called in his senior officers to discuss the dubious option of abandoning the river and seeking to evade Canby by taking a detour through the mountains. Sibley, according to Lieutenant Phillip Fulcrod, favored continuing down the river, but Green, Bethel Coopwood, the commander of the "San Elizandro Spy Company," and Henry C. McNeill, the lieutenant colonel of the Fifth Texas, an 1857 graduate of West Point, and a veteran of service with the old army in New Mexico Territory prior to the war, urged the mountain route. Scurry refused to give it an opinion.[25]

When Sibley's retrograde movement began, a severe lack of horses and mules dictated that each company could be allowed only one wagon, and, yet more demoralizing, a number of artillery pieces had to be left behind. Now once again, on April 17, at their camp on the Puerco River about forty-five miles above Craig, the Texans "burnt and destroyed everything we had this morning except blankets, cooking utensils, a suit of clothes, and overcoats." In the face of imminent disaster, Sibley ordered the men to prepare ten days' rations and to prepare to travel. With mules packed with seven days' rations and with "blankets and a frying pan and coffee pot," the brigade began an arduous—some thought impossible—march through the mountainous desert.[26]

Two weeks earlier, a small party of Coopwood's Spy Company, recruited at Mesilla and therefore familiar with the terrain and its few water holes, had located a route that would take the Confederates through the Magdalena and San Mateo Mountains, on a detour forty miles to the west of Fort Craig. On the evening of April 17, with Coopwood as its guide, the command departed the Rio Grande and headed into the mountains. "Now," wrote Peticolas, "commenced one of the most remarkable retreats ever heard of." Leaving "all our most valuable articles scattered over the ground in profusion," the fugitive brigade marched until at 2:00 AM when it reached a small lake, called Salt Pond on account of the brackishness of the water, at the northern end of the Sierra Magdalena range. There it camped for the remainder of the night.[27]

Canby made no effort to pursue, and on the eighteenth a Union diarist recorded that "we can see nothing of the Texans today." Instead, they pushed on toward Fort Craig, marching that day about fifteen miles before encamping in a large bottom, where "there was little water and less wood." Hollister claims that Canby was aware that the Confederates were "slipping like eels through our fingers," but made no effort to cut them off, and from that point discontinued his pursuit, with the exception of Captain James "Paddy" Graydon's company, which merely followed at a distance. At this point, Sibley appears to have virtually abdicated command of the brigade in favor of Green and Scurry, who assumed responsibility for its leadership. At daybreak in the Rebel camp, Scurry sounded a cheerful reveille, calling, "Come, boys, it's only four miles to breakfast; let's go and get it!" So the men packed the remaining mules and started down the sandy canyon. "The four miles proved to be about eight before we walked it, and a good many of us were nearly broken down when we made a stop." Not until noon did they come to water, the aptly named Rio Salado, a sink that was, according to Lieutenant Julius Giesecke, "so salty that we could hardly use it for coffee." The next water was twenty-five miles away.[28]

At last the men camped at Ojo del Pueblo, near present-day Magdalena, New Mexico. "We supped heartily of bread and coffee, our only diet now, and fell asleep." To add to their growing catalogue of calamity, measles had broken out among the troops, and Peticolas noted in his journal that "smallpox begins to prevail to a considerable extent amongst the soldiers, and pneumonia also."[29]

On the nineteenth, while the Federals rested in camp to recruit their horses and mules, the Texans moved from their camp on the Rio Salado to Bear Spring. "We have no road," wrote Peticolas, and the brigade was forced to abandon the last of its wheeled vehicles and its excess artillery ammunition, and possibly left three howitzers. But although there was "some talk of spiking the artillery and leaving it," the brigade refused to abandon the fine guns of the McRae Battery, captured at Valverde. Green and Scurry, regarding them as symbols of the heroic but doomed sacrifice of the brigade, were determined to "take them through a wild, broken, mountainous country for ninety miles where never wheel ran before."[30]

Upon reaching one extremely steep hill, Scurry dismounted and called for volunteers to manhandle the artillery to the summit, taking hold of a cannon rope himself. "Men flocked to the piece," said Peticolas, and all five of the guns were drawn to the top of the hill. Thereafter, each company was made responsible for one a canon. With "colonels, captains, and all, working alike, everyone determined that those guns should go through," over hills and valleys that "a horseman would have thought impassable," the Texans returned to Fort Bliss with nine pieces of artillery, including the Valverde Battery, which served them for the remainder of the war.[31]

After another day of murderous fatigue, without water and often pulling artillery pieces up steep hills, the brigade reached the crest of the pass between the Magdalena and San Mateo ranges at about sundown, still six miles from water. "No order was observed, no company stayed together, the wearied sank down upon the grass, regardless of the cold, to rest and sleep," Peticolas later remembered. "The strong, with words of execration upon their lips, pressed feverishly and frantically on for water. Dozens fell in together and in despair gave up all hope of getting to water and stopped, built fires and fell asleep . . . and on, on struggled the main column, through scenery the grandest and most picturesque imaginable."[32]

On the twentieth, while the Rebels continued their grueling trek through the San Mateo Mountains, Canby's column crossed the Rio Grande at Limitar and was overtaken by a commissary train from Fort Union before going into camp at sundown. Ironically, two Southern diarists recorded that their commissary was enriched by two antelope and a 400-pound bear, killed by some of the men. The following day the Confederate column, "crawling along the side of the mountain," passed a waterless day in sight of Fort Craig, and after forty miles of climbing "a high steep hill, dragging up the nine heavy guns," struck camp in a narrow canyon a mile from water. "Poor fellows!" wrote Hollister. In a remarkably charitable passage from the man who, only two months earlier had called for a war of extermination, he observed that "they are our brothers, erring, it may be," and invoked "a passing tear for the brave dead. . . . Any cause that men sustain to death becomes sacred, at least, to them. Surely we can afford to pay a tribute to the courage and nobleness that prefers death to even *fancied* enthrallment."[33]

The retreating Texans started early on the morning of April 22 and soon reached East Red Canyon, a seemingly impassible barrier. But locking the wheels of the guns and holding fast to the drag ropes, the men slid them down the slope and then dragged them up the other side. By then, every canteen in the brigade was empty, and as Peticolas wrote with rare understatement, the men "soon began to suffer for want of it." Late in the evening, after a twenty-five-mile ordeal, they arrived at Alamosa Creek, flowing with the best and most abundant water that the brigade has seen since leaving the Rio Grande. "With lips black and parched, and throats swelled and dry," the men dashed down the canyon sides, where they threw themselves into the stream. "Oh, the water, the good water!!" Peticolas exalted.[34]

William Steele

Steele, to whom Tom Green referred as "a distinguished dragoon of the old army," was born in New York in 1820, and in 1840 he graduated from West Point, thirty-first in his class of forty-two. As a second lieutenant of the Second U.S. Dragoons, he took part in the war in Florida against the Seminole Indians, and in the Mexican War saw action at Palo Alto and Monterrey under Zachary Taylor and later under Winfield Scott in the Mexico City campaign, receiving a brevet promotion to captain for gallant and meritorious conduct at the battles of Contreras and Churubusco. After considerable service against the Indians on the western frontier from Texas to the Dakota Territory, during which he rose to the rank of captain, Steele resigned from the U.S. Army on May 30, 1861, and on October 4, 1861, was commissioned as colonel of the Seventh Texas Mounted Rifles. Although assigned to the Army of New Mexico, he did not take a direct role in the campaign up the Rio Grande, remaining instead in command of the troops occupying the El Paso–Mesilla area. Upon Sibley's departure for Richmond at the end of the campaign, Steele remained as civil governor and military commander of Arizona Territory until his promotion to brigadier general in September 1862 and assignment to the command of the Department of Indian Territory. Superseded by Brigadier General Samuel Bell Maxey in December 1863, he was assigned to the command of the defenses of Galveston until the spring of 1864 when he took part in the Red River campaign as a brigade commander in Major General Tom Green's Cavalry division, which he briefly commanded after Green's death at the battle of Blair's Landing. Following the war, Steele returned to Texas, where, from 1866 to 1873, he engaged in the mercantile business in San Antonio. With the end of Reconstruction in Texas, he was appointed as adjutant general, serving from 1874 to 1879, during which time he oversaw the reorganization of the Texas Rangers. Steele died in San Antonio on January 12, 1885.

On the twenty-third, the brigade managed eighteen or twenty miles with "only three very steep high mountains to work our artillery over," and made camp with neither food nor water. The following day the men found water in Hondo Creek, cooked, and "ate heartily, as our long fast justified us in doing," but only on bread and coffee, their only diet for the past five days. There they spent the entire day, resting from their long ordeal, and on the twenty-fifth arrived in the valley of the Rio Grande about forty miles below Fort Craig. There they "ate their last bread without knowing when we would again get some flour," but near Alamosa they found about 150 sheep and eight work oxen. On April 27, the Sibley brigade met Colonel Steele and the Third Texas Mounted Rifles, who had arrived from San Antonio too late to take part in the campaign, with seven wagonloads of provisions. "We all ate heartily of bread and coffee," Peticolas reported, "but got nothing else brought us." At last, on April 28, Sibley's struggling column reached the relative ease and safety of Fort Thorn. There, typically, Sibley abandoned his command and rode on to Fort Bliss. He remained there but a few days, however, for on hearing of the rapid approach of Colonel James H. Carleton's California Column, he left for San Antonio, utterly abandoning his men.[35]

In nine days, the Army of New Mexico had journeyed 150 miles through some of the most unforgiving terrain in the desert Southwest. Captain Graydon, whose company followed the Sibley Brigade through the mountains, found three fresh graves and reported that the Confederates had "burned up about nineteen wagons, ten ambulances, six caissons, and three carriages" and destroyed six 100-pound barrels of powder as well as a great deal of camp equipage. In addition, they abandoned one 12-pounder howitzer and two mountain howitzers. "The road from Ojo del Pueblo is strewn with old harness, iron ovens, and in fact everything but small ammunition," he reported. "It seems they destroyed very little if any, of that." Passing over the same route a year later," Pettis reported that he "not infrequently found a piece of a gun-carriage, or part of a harness, or some piece of camp or garrison equipage, with occasionally a white, dry skeleton of a man. At some points it seemed impossible for men to have made their way."[36]

Once again, had Canby, whose column had arrived at Fort Craig the evening that the Texans reached Alamosa Creek, moved to interdict the remnant of the Army of New Mexico, the Texans would have had no choice but to surrender. Colonels Paul and Chivington wished to pursue, but Canby would not consent. "We have undoubtedly seen the last of them," wrote Hollister, "and our active campaign, having continued some two months, has come to an end for the present."[37]

Adding to the Rebels' discomfiture was the rapid approach of Carleton's California Column. After with great difficulty amassing thousands of tons of food, forage, ammunition, and equipment at Fort Yuma, late in February 1862 the first of the 2,350 men and hundreds of horses and mules began the trek from San Diego to the Rio Grande, marching in company-sized units to minimize their impact on the barren desert's scant water resources. Not until April 15, at Picacho Pass, a station on the Butterfield Overland Mail about forty-five miles northwest of Tucson, did the vanguard of the California Column encounter Confederate troops of Captain Sherrod Hunter's command. Carleton's Pima scouts reported the presence of a ten-man Rebel picket post guarding the pass, and twenty-five California cavalrymen were detached to capture them, thus opening the final descent into Tucson.[38]

In the ensuing skirmish—the westernmost engagement of Union and Confederate troops during the Civil War—a dozen mounted Federals charged the surprised Rebels, capturing three of them. But quickly rallying, the Southerners opened fire from a thicket, killing the lieutenant in charge of the Union detachment. In a firefight that lasted more than an hour, two more Federals were killed and three wounded. The Confederates suffered no further casualties, but withdrew toward Tucson. Five days later, on May 20, the California Column occupied Tucson, which Carleton saw as the key to Arizona Territory. In the Confederate sympathizers taken prisoner there, Private John W. Teal of the Second California Cavalry found to be "a true type of southern chivalry which is composed of bone, sinew, skin and any amount of ignorant conceit."[39]

On April 27, Lieutenant Colonel Scurry received orders to return to Texas to raise a new regiment and departed at daybreak of the day following after delivering a farewell address and turning over command of the First Texas Mounted Rifles to Colonel Reily, who had just returned from his diplomatic mission to the governors of Chihuahua and Sonora.

Sherrod Hunter

Hunter was born on March 5, 1834, in Fayetteville, Lincoln County, Tennessee. Orphaned in August 1840, his childhood was spent in the households of various relatives. He operated the firm of Goodrich and Hunter, a grocery business in Fayetteville, until March 1857. Leaving Tennessee, he arrived in New Mexico Territory sometime between 1857 and 1859, settling first in Mesilla and then moving to a farm on the Mimbres River, about twenty-five miles north of the present-day town of Deming.

When John R. Baylor called for volunteers to defend the newly created Confederate Territory, Hunter enlisted at Mesilla in Captain George Frazer's Company of Arizona Rangers and was soon elected as the company's first lieutenant, and when Baylor raised a regiment of Arizona Rangers for frontier defense, he commissioned Hunter as captain of Company A. The Mesilla *Times* of January 18, 1862, editorialized that "we do not know of a single officer under whom we would rather serve, nor one who has more compleetly [sic] the confidence and respect of his men, than he has."

On February 10, 1862, Hunter was ordered to Tucson, Arizona, to establish an advanced military post for observation of Union forces known to be gathering in California, and to pacify the surrounding area, which was under threat of attack by the Apache. In Tucson, Hunter conducted a hit-and-run campaign in which his company removed almost all Federal troops from the present state of Arizona and carried the Confederate flag to within eighty miles of the Colorado River, which was the farthest western penetration of the Confederate army. He further captured or destroyed supplies gathered for the use of the Union force then advancing from California, thus delaying its advance for more than a month, and winning the westernmost military action of the Civil War at Picacho Pass on April 15, 1862. They were forced to evacuate Tucson on May 14, 1862, falling back on Mesilla, and accompanied Henry Hopkins Sibley's retreat to San Antonio.

On October 3, 1862, Hunter was promoted to the rank of major of Colonel George W. Baylor's Second Cavalry Regiment, Arizona Brigade. Hunter played a prominent part in the campaigns in south Louisiana in 1863 and the Red River campaign of 1864, most notably the capture of Brashear City, Louisiana, on June 22, 1864.

On January 25, 1865, the Confederate War Department authorized Hunter to raise a regiment for service in Arizona and New Mexico, apparently with the rank of colonel, although no extant document verifies that assumption. In any event, the war had ended before the regiment could be raised, and Hunter joined the movement to form a Confederate colony at Cordova, near Vera Cruz, but on May 11, 1866, he left Mexico to return to his former home in Lincoln County, Tennessee. Thereafter nothing is known about his life, and the date and place of his death are not recorded.

With Scurry's departure, wrote Peticolas, "we lost the best officer, most polished gentleman, most sociable gentleman, and the most popular colonel in the whole outfit." With Scurry went Coopwood, who had been commissioned as major of the new regiment yet to be raised. Peticolas characterized Coopwood as "a brave man, a good fighter, and deserves promotion for successfully guiding the brigade through the mountains around Craig."[40]

Much less popular with the men was Sibley. According to Peticolas, the general was "heartily despised by every man in the brigade for his want of feeling, poor generalship, and cowardice," and all had determined never to return to New Mexico unless "under a different general." In reference to his having notoriously ejected a sick soldier from his wagon on the retreat to Fort Bliss, Peticolas charged that "several Mexican whores can find room to ride in his wagon while the poor private soldier is thrown out to die on the way." Perhaps more damning to the Texans, Sergeant Starr observed in a letter to his father that "among the soldiers I hear ridicule and curses heaped upon the head of our general. They call him a coward, which appears very plausible too, for he has never been in an engagement or where there was any appearance of going to be one." Moreover, he maintained, Sibley's "bad management has been the cause of our ruin."[41]

Almost alone in his defense of Sibley was Theophilus Noel, who believed the commander to be "a high minded, noble, valorous and gifted officer, endowed with a principle too lofty and honorable to deign to any acts calculated to wrong anyone, let him be whom he may." Even the loyal Noel, however, believed that the campaign had been "defeated from want of supplies and reinforcements," the former of which, at least may be directly attributable to Sibley. As he observed with wry understatement, "the territory which we occupied was no storehouse," and Canby's scorched earth strategy had been fully enforced before Sibley moved to secure the supplies that he had promised. More succinctly, Starr felt that the Texans had been "starved out, not run out."[42]

The men of the once powerful Army of New Mexico marched slowly for Fort Bliss, strung out in a column fifty miles long. "We are slowly recruiting by traveling this easy journey," wrote Peticolas, and occasionally some soldier could be heard "humming a tune, some familiar air or favorite love song, but often the tune stops when memory brings back some remembrance of our hardships, and then the singer seems for a few minutes ashamed of his cheerfulness." In general, however, "a better trend of feeling and more cheerfulness" had begun to characterize the brigade, and "faces look less care worn and elongated."[43]

By May 5, they began arriving at Fort Bliss in squads, but even then their troubles were far from over. On May 7, Mother Magdalen Hayden wrote to another member of her order that the sisters of the Loretto Academy "could hear them passing all night," their convent being on one of El Paso's main streets. "Some came on horseback, others on foot," she wrote, "and others were almost dragged to the city. All were in a most needy and destitute condition in regard to the common necessities of life." Although a wagon train from Victoria was expected daily, on May 11, Peticolas and his comrades were still "lying in camp eating scant rations and wishing for a change of clothes." The region had long since been drained of all of its surplus, Starr wrote to his father, "and our supply of subsistence stores is not very great."[44]

The wagons arrived from Victoria on the thirteenth, and "boxes were opened; numerous packages were directed to individuals and a quantity of clothing sent to the company." Peticolas rejoiced in receiving "two or three packages, touching though useful reminders of dear ones at home." Best of all, perhaps, he reported going down to the Rio Grande to take "a thorough bath" and put on clean clothes. "What a luxury!"[45]

At Fort Bliss, Sibley issued a proclamation to the soldiers of the Army of New Mexico, expressing his "unfeigned pride and pleasure" in congratulating them on the "successes which have crowned their arms in the many encounters with the enemy during the short but brilliant campaign which has just terminated," and assuring them that their performances at Valverde, Glorieta, Albuquerque, and Peralta would be "duly chronicled, and form one of the brightest pages in the history of the Second American Revolution." Starr, for one, was less than sure. Every man involved in the campaign "detests the country so much that they are really glad to go," he wrote, but at the same time it pained him to leave, because he believed that, despite Sibley's assurances to the contrary, "our operations out here will all be lost in history," with New Orleans having fallen and the battle of Shiloh having been fought at the very time that the brigade was fighting at Albuquerque and Peralta and suffering the horrors of its retreat across the mountains around Fort Craig.[46]

Although the soldiers would almost surely have agreed with Sibley's assessment that "the boasted valor of Texans has been fully vindicated," his reference to their "successful and almost unprecedented evacuation" surely reminded them that the campaign might have been a success had it been properly managed. That same week, for example, Starr wrote to his father from Fort Bliss that Charles Mansfield Raguet, a lieutenant in the artillery, was going home, "intending to find service in a better country under a better general. He, like many more of us, is disgusted with such *generalship* and *management* as marked our course."[47]

By the final week of May, Captain Alexander wrote to a friend that "for the first time, so far as concerns my body, [I] feel comfortable and rested since this Brigade left San Antonio." By then, as well, the Sibley Brigade had scraped together enough provisions to commence its seven-hundred-mile return march. Even then, transportation was scarce, and Peticolas complained of having to sell one of his blankets to make his baggage lighter, "though it weighs very little."[48]

"Words can hardly express how much I dread to undertake to walk across the vast desert region between Fort Quitman and Fort Clark," he lamented. "It was hard enough riding it in the fall, but walking it in the blazing sun of a torrid summer, it will be infinitely worse." Alexander told a friend that "I walked all over N. M. and can take another jaunt, although I must confess I do not like the business," and Starr agreed that the brigade would "have hard times perhaps before we reach San Antonio. The prospect of walking from here to that place is not very inviting." By the time it reached home, Peticolas predicted, the brigade will have "dwindled to a regiment."[49]

From May 20 to mid-June, leaving only four hundred men of Steele’s regiment to hold the Fort Bliss–Mesilla area and maintain the Confederate Territory of Arizona, the Sibley Brigade marched for home by the same stage road they had used seven months earlier coming west. As they had the previous winter, the regiments marched in dispersed battalions to find sufficient water on the way. From Fort Bliss to Fort Davis to Fort Stockton to Fort Lancaster, across the Devil’s River to Fort Clark, across the Nueces at Uvalde, they struggled across the desert, having at times to push and pull their wagons through the heavy sand, with the number of sick making the effort “extremely laborious to those who are well.” Each day’s march became a struggle to reach water, and Indians ran off livestock and polluted wells.[50]

Canby, now with two thousand men at Fort Craig, seemed content to let them depart in peace. Hollister reported “some preparation and much talk of an expedition going down to the Mesilla to drive the balance of the Texans home,” but not until the last days of July did five companies of the Colorado Volunteers and eight of the Fifth U.S. Infantry start for Mesilla, and after three days’ march, they were recalled. By then, Canby had been transferred to staff duties in the East, and Carleton, also promoted to brigadier, succeeded him as commander of the Department of New Mexico. Steele, hopelessly outnumbered and without logistical support, evacuated Confederate Arizona and withdrew his last troops from the Fort Bliss area by July 12.[51]

On July 19, the leading elements of the Army of New Mexico reached San Antonio to receive a sixty-day furlough to rest, recruit, and reequip themselves with horses, clothing, blankets, and “such supplies as they could obtain from their friends and relatives at home.” Then, the men hoped, their brigade would be transferred to a theater in which it could “render some efficient service to our country.” New Mexico “has proven itself a land of sorrow to us,” Sergeant Starr wrote “for our little band has been much reduced by disease and battle.”[52]

Total numbers of killed in action, dead of disease or starvation, wounded, captured, and missing are impossible now to calculate.

Lieutenant Giesecke estimated that fewer than two thousand men returned to San Antonio, seventeen hundred fewer than the brigade had left with, only seven months before. Other historians have calculated that Sibley suffered about one thousand casualties, one-half of whom died. Almost all of the Confederate wounded fell into Union hands when the Army of New Mexico retreated out of the territory. Of the brigade's field grade officers, four had been killed, Lieutenant Colonel John S. Sutton and Major Samuel A. Lockridge at Valverde, and Majors Henry Raguet and John S. Shropshire at Glorieta.[53]

Discontent among the soldiers was great, and the New Mexico campaign, all agreed, had been a debacle. The territory was "not worth the loss of lives and money necessary for its conquest," Starr averred. "I do not think it is worth the life of a single Texian." Captain Jerome B. McCown, concurred precisely. "We are all tired of this country, and are all anxious to return to the sunny land of Texas." There, he wrote, the soldiers would be defending their own homes and families and not "throwing our lives away in endeavoring to obtain possession of a country which is not worth the life of one good man."[54]

In a mournful epitaph for the New Mexico campaign, Starr wrote to his father that he had "lost all interest in, or care for the country." The only benefits arising from the campaign were "the name of our victories, the fine battery of six guns taken from the enemy of Val Verde, and the 800 or a 1000 stand of small arms." Despite the fact that the brigade had left San Antonio poorly equipped for such a campaign, "what we had has all been lost," wagons, one half of its horses, "and everything else but the clothes we had on our backs." Somewhat more bitterly, Captain Alexander lamented that "we have to return to Texas without having benefited our country one dime's worth."[55]

Despite their grief over their losses and their bitterness over their general's poor leadership, the men of the Sibley Brigade remained confident in each other and in their field grade and company grade officers who, Starr maintained, "one at all, have, in battle, shown themselves gallant, brave men. Always in the front where the balls flew thickest."

The "unfortunate result of this campaign," he insisted, had not been the result of any "failure on the part of the soldiers in the performance of their duty," they having in every instance "shown themselves to be true Texans, true to each other, true to our cause."[56]

Alexander boasted that "we gave the Yankees the devil in every fight up the country," and Starr remained satisfied that "at anytime and anywhere, so we have ammunition, we can whip them." But according to Senator Williamson Simpson Oldham of Texas, "the wild-goose Sibley expedition" had merely left 3,500 of his state's best troops "to perish on the arid plains of New Mexico, and they have only drawn the enemy upon our frontier, ready to come down upon us this winter." Rather, Oldham believed, they should have been deployed with Major General Thomas C. Hindman's army in Arkansas and used to liberate Missouri. There, he told the Confederate Senate, they "might have raised a hundred thousand men, seized St. Louis, and thus drawn the Federal armies out of Tennessee and Kentucky."[57]

With the California Brigade in firm control of the Mesilla Valley, the men of the First Colorado were freed for duty elsewhere. Following a reconnaissance mission into northwest Texas in the winter of 1862–1863, General Carleton wrote to John Evans, who had succeeded William Gilpin as governor of Colorado, that he did not believe any considerable force from there would attempt to invade New Mexico again, at least for the present. "That the so-called Southern Confederacy, looking to a permanent separation from the Union, will desire to have a strip of territory extending across the continent to cover the silver and gold fields of Arizona and to have a port on the Pacific there cannot be a doubt; and that there will be a strong effort made to this end sooner or later." Citing Union reverses in the East, he predicted that a second Confederate attempt was "more than probable," but believed that chances for such an attempt being made in the immediate future were so remote as to warrant sending the Colorado volunteers home.[58]

These orders did not displease the "Colorados." Hollister and his comrades had long considered the territory to be desolate. To him, New

Mexico, with its "mountains, sand hills, and arid wastes; the whole poorly supplied with running water, and, owing to almost total absence of rain, but scantily clothed with the vegetation," had never been anything other than an expense. Therefore, when ordered back to Fort Union, he wrote, the men of his regiment were "anxious to make it a little more so and leave the centipedes and tarantulas unmolested in the undisputed possession of this part of the territory of New Mexico. No prisoner ever left a cell with more delight, or less regret than we have left this horrible place, as we bid adieu to Camp Val Verde and its surrounding desert."[59]

However desolate New Mexico might have been, and however badly Sibley handled his campaign there, his vision had not been entirely false. With the Confederate failure to hold New Mexico, the South lost its only opportunity to create a connecting link between the Atlantic and Pacific Oceans, along what was then thought to be the only practicable transcontinental railroad route. It lost valuable agricultural and grazing lands into which slavery might have spread, as well as one of the richest mineral regions in world.[60]

But was such an occupation possible? Certainly the immediate capture of Fort Craig after the battle of Valverde and a rapid strike up the Rio Grande to capture Federal stores at Albuquerque and Santa Fe would have greatly strengthened the Army of New Mexico, made the capture of Fort Union probable, and allowed the Confederates to face the First Colorado Volunteers on more than equal terms. Had the brigade been able to accomplish Sibley's grandiose vision of crossing the deserts of Arizona and California and reaching San Diego and Los Angeles, the American Civil War might well have had a different outcome. Had such a possibility truly existed, then Anderson's assessment that "the conflict in New Mexico should be regarded as one of the decisive campaigns of the war," would have been unquestionably accurate. Even with Fort Union in Confederate hands, however, Carleton's California Column marching for Mesilla and a large force of Kansas volunteers, then forming at Fort Leavenworth, would have almost surely forced the Confederates out of the territory.[61]

Notes

Chapter 1

1. George Archibald McCall, *New Mexico in 1850: A Military View* (Robert W. Frazer, ed., Norman: University of Oklahoma Press, 1968), 3, 20, 27; James A. Albert, *Albert's New Mexico Report, 1846–1847* (Albuquerque: Horne and Wallace), 1962. For the fullest treatment of the New Mexico Campaign of 1862, see Donald S. Frazier, *Blood and Treasure: Confederate Empire in the Southwest* (College Station: Texas A&M University Press, 1995). Also useful are Martin Hardwick Hall, *Sibley's New Mexico Campaign* (Austin: University of Texas Press, 1960; reprint, Albuquerque: University of New Mexico Press, 2000) and Robert Lee Kerby, *The Confederate Invasion of New Mexico and Arizona, 1861–1862* (San Jose, Calif.: Westlore, 1958).
2. Henderson K. Yoakum, *History of Texas: From Its First Settlement in 1685 to Its Annexation to the United States in 1846* (New York: Redfield, 1855), 526–528; *Laws of the Republic of Texas* (Houston, 1838), 133–134; *Senate Executive Document* number 52, First Session, Thirtieth Congress, 1847, 71–80.
3. "Treaty of Peace, Friendship, Limits, and Settlement between the United States of America and the Mexican Republic," *United States Statutes at Large*, vol. IX, 922–942.
4. *Texas House Journal*, Third Legislature, Extra Session (Austin 1850), 6–18; Ernest Wallace and David M. Vigness, eds., *Documents of Texas History* (Austin: The Steck Company, 1960), 179–180.
5. *Congressional Globe*, 31: 1, 871, 1013 and 1714; Amelia W. Williams and Eugene Barker, eds., *The Writings of Sam Houston, 1813–1863* (Austin: Jenkins Publishing Company, 1970), V, 181. See also *Congressional Globe*, 29 September 1850, 31: 1, App. 1714; Thomas W. Cutrer, ed., "'A Lion in Her Path': Texas, New Mexico, and the United States Army, 1850, *Military History of the West*, XXXIV, (2005), 75–80.
6. *O.R.*, IV, 23. See also Jason H. Silverman, "Confederate Ambitions for the Southwest: A New Perspective," *Red River Valley Historical Review*, IV (winter 1979), 62–71.
7. *O.R.*, IV, 96; William Davidson in Jerry Thompson, ed., *Civil War in the Southwest: Recollections of the Sibley Brigade* (College Station: Texas A&M University Press, 2001), 3–4.
8. James Cooper McKee, *Narrative of the Surrender of a Command of the U.S. Forces at Fort Fillmore New Mexico in July, A.D. 1861, with Related Reports by John R. Baylor, C.S.A., and Others* (Boston, 1886; Houston: Stagecoach Press, 1960), 6–7; anonymous soldier quoted in Lamar, *The Far Southwest*, 110; quoted in Silverman, "Confederate Ambitions for the Southwest," 66.
9. Quoted in William A. Keleher, *Turmoil in New Mexico, 1846–1868* (Santa Fe: Rydal Press, 1952), 394; Horace Greeley, *The American Conflict: A History of the Great Rebellion in the United States of America, 1860–1865* (Hartford, Conn.: O. D. Case and Company, 1867), II, 19.
10. T. T. Teel, "Sibley's New Mexican Campaign—Its Objects and the Causes of Its Failure," *Battles and Leaders of the Civil War*, II, 700.
11. Santa Fe *Gazette*, 2 February 1861.
12. *O.R.*, IV, 39.
13. *O.R.*, IX, 634–635.

14. Hattie M. Anderson, ed., "With the Confederates in New Mexico during the Civil War–Memoirs of Hank Smith," *Panhandle-Plains Historical Review* II (1929), 65–97.
15. *O.R.*, supplement, 492–493; *O.R.*, I, I, 604.
16. Ovando James Hollister, *History of the First Colorado Volunteers* (Denver: Thomas Gibson & Co., 1863), reprinted as *Colorado Volunteers in New Mexico, 1862* (Chicago, Ill.: Lakeside Press 1962), 163–164; Nolie Mumey, ed., *Bloody Trails along the Rio Grande: A Day-By-Day Diary of Alonzo Ferdinand Ickis 1836–1917: A Soldier and His Activities with Company B; the First Volunteer Regiment to Leave the Territory of Colorado for the Civil War: Their Participation in the Battle of Valverede, New Mexico* (Denver: Old West Publishing Co., 1958), 69–70.
17. *O.R.*, IV, 65; Santa Fe *Gazette*, 23 February 1861.
18. *O.R.*, IV, I, 57. For an examination of the two regiments of New Mexico volunteers in the Rio Grande campaign, see Jerry Don Thompson, "Mexican Americans in the Civil War: The Battle of Valverde," *Texana*, X, 1, (1972), 1–19.
19. *O.R.*, XV, 576; McKee, *Narrative*, 6; Allen Latham Anderson, "Canby's Services in the New Mexican Campaign," in Robert Underwood Johnson and Clarence Clough Buel, eds., *Battles and Leaders of the Civil War* (New York: The Century Co., 1887-1888), II, 698–699; *O.R.*, IV, 69.
20. Hollister, *History of the First Regiment of Colorado Volunteers*, reprinted as Richard Harwell, ed., *Colorado Volunteers in New Mexico, 1862* (Chicago: The Lakeside Press, 1962), 4–5.
21. Hollister, *History of the First Regiment of Colorado Volunteers*, 6, 15.
22. Anderson, "Canby's Services in the New Mexican Campaign," 697.
23. Josiah Royce, *California, From the Conquest in 1846 to the Second Vigilance Committee in San Francisco: A Study of American Character* (Boston: Houghton Mifflin, 1886), 392–393; Leonard L. Richards, *The California Gold Rush and the Coming of the Civil War* (New York: Knopf, 2007).
24. George Gwyther, "Our Scout to Black Cañon," *Overland Monthly and Out West Magazine*, V, 3 (September 1870), 222.
25. Jerry D. Thompson, ed., *From Desert to Bayou: The Civil War Journal and Sketches of Morgan Wolfe Merrick* (El Paso: Texas Western Press, 1991), 25; *O.R.*, IV, 51.
26. George H. Pettis, "The Confederate Invasion of New Mexico and Arizona," in Robert Underwood Johnson and Clarence Clough Buel, eds., *Battles and Leaders of the Civil War* (New York: The Century Co., 1887-1888), II, 103; McKee, *Narrative*, 7–8.
27. Jerry Don Thompson, *John Robert Baylor: Texas Indian Fighter and Confederate Soldier* (Hillsboro, Tex.: Hill Junior College Press, 1971).
28. Martin Hardwick Hall, ed., "The Taylor Letters: Confederate Correspondence from Fort Bliss, 1861," *Military History of Texas and the Southwest*, XV, 2 (1979), 55; Thompson, ed., *From Desert to Bayou*, 24.

Chapter 2

1. Thompson, ed., *From Desert to Bayou*, 18; Milam Taylor to Charles S. Taylor, 7 July 1861, in Hall, ed., "The Taylor Letters," 54.
2. Thompson, ed., *From Desert to Bayou*, 19.
3. Thompson, ed., *From Desert to Bayou*, 24; John R. Baylor, 21 September 1861, *O.R.*, IV, 17; Pettis, "The Confederate Invasion of New Mexico and Arizona," 103; Enrique B. D'Hamel, *The Adventures of a Tenderfoot: History of the 2nd Regt. Mounted Rifles and Co. G, 33rd Regt. and Capt. Coopwood's Spy Co and 2nd Texas in Texas and New Mexico* (Waco: W. M. Morrison Books, 1965), 8.

According to one of their number, Enrique B. D'Hamel, himself a Cuban, "all the members of the company were Texas backwoodsmen, ranchers and cowboys who knew the country from San Antonio to Santa Fe, New Mexico, and from mountain to mountain on both sides of the Rio Grande River. Most of the men had been Indian fighters." Another wrote that the company consisted of sixty-four men who were "ripe for any adventure, however daring or desperate. They were all Texans and many of them bore the scars of many fierce conflicts with the Indians and border ruffians." S. W. Merchant, "Fighting with Sibley in New Mexico," *Hunter's Magazine* 1 (November, 1910), 7.

4. Hall, ed., "The Taylor Letters," 56–57.
5. McKee, *Narrative*, 8–14; Hall, ed., "The Taylor Letters," 56–57.
6. Thompson, ed., *From Desert to Bayou*, 25; William S. Kiser, *Turmoil on the Rio Grande: History of the Mesilla Valley, 1846–1865* (College Station: Texas A&M University Press, 2001); *O.R.*, IV, 17–20; Lydia Spencer Lane, *I Married a Soldier or Old Days in the Old Army* (Albuquerque: Horn and Wallace, 1964), 107–110; Thompson, *John Robert Baylor*, 28–34.
7. McKee, *Narrative*, 25; Thompson, ed., *Civil War in the Southwest*, 15.
8. According to Merrick's account, Baylor said that he would "fight first, and surrender afterwards," and McKee recorded that the reply was that "if he wished to take the town, to come and take it." Hall, ed., "The Taylor Letters," 58; Thompson, ed., *From Desert to Bayou*, 110; McKee, *Narrative*, 18; *O.R.*, IV, 57–58.
9. D'Hamel, *The Adventures of a Tenderfoot*, 10; McKee, *Narrative*, 20.
10. John R. Baylor to T. A. Washington, 21 September 1861, *O.R.*, IV, 17–20; Lynde to Acting Assistant Adjutant-General, 26 July 1861, *O.R.*, IV, 4–5; Hall, ed., "The Taylor Letters," 58; Martin Hardwick Hall, "The Skirmish at Mesilla," *Arizona and the West*, I, 4, (Winter 1959), 343–351; McKee, *Narrative*, 21.
11. McNally's statement was made at the at official investigation of Lynde's actions on the lower Rio Grande in July 1861, held at Jefferson Barracks, Missouri, later that year. *O.R.* IV, 13; McKee, *Narrative*, 4.
12. *O.R.*, IV, 58; McKee, *Narrative*, 4.
13. *O.R.*, IV, 6.
14. "They tried to fire some of the houses, but our company was into the post in time to put out the fire before much damage was done," recorded Sergeant Merrick. "They had run a trail of powder out in a magazine that connected with several kegs of powder on the inside. Why they didn't fire it I don't know." McKee, *Narrative*, 23–24; Thompson, ed., *Desert to Bayou*, 25; *O.R.*, IV, 4–6.
15. *O.R.*, IV, 5–20; McKee, *Narrative*, 26.
16. Anderson, ed., "Memoirs of Hank Smith," 78.
17. *O.R.*, IV, 6.
18. Gibbs to Canby, 6 August 1861, quoted in McKee, *Narrative*, 50.
19. *O.R.*, IV, 10.
20. *O.R.*, IV, 10–11; McKee, *Narrative*, 21–22, 29–30; D'Hamel, *The Adventures of a Tenderfoot*, 11.
21. *O.R.*, IV, 6.
22. McKee, *Narrative*, 31; *O.R.*, IV, 6, 11, 37, 44, 45, 50, 56, 58, 60. For a more sympathetic analysis of Lynde's character and actions, see A. F. H. Armstrong, "The Case of Major Isaac Lynde," *New Mexico Historical Review*, XXXVI, 1 (January 1961), 1–22.
23. Thompson, ed., *From Desert to Bayou*, 25.

24. Thompson, ed., *From Desert to Bayou*, 28.
25. *O.R.*, Series IV, I, 791–793; Pettis, "The Confederate Invasion of New Mexico and Arizona," 102, 104–105; *O.R.*, IV, 20–21.
26. Thompson, ed., *From Desert to Bayou*, 25; *O.R.*, Series IV, volume I, 791–792.
27. *O.R.*, Series IV, volume I, 792–793.
28. *O.R.*, Series IV, volume I, 792; Pettis, "The Confederate Invasion of New Mexico and Arizona" 104.
29. Hollister, *History of the First Colorado Volunteers*, 170–171; Pettis, "The Confederate Invasion of New Mexico and Arizona," 103; Michael L. Tate, ed., "A Johnny Reb and in Sibley's New Mexico Campaign: Reminiscences of Pvt. Henry C. Wright, 1861–1862," part one, *East Texas Historical Journal*, XXV, 2 (1988), 31.
30. Pettis, "The Confederate Invasion of New Mexico and Arizona," 104; *O.R.*, IV, 26–32; Thompson, ed., *Westward the Texans*, 132; Hall, ed., "The Taylor Letters," 57–58; Thompson, ed., *From Desert to Bayou*, 112.
31. Thompson, ed., *From Desert to Bayou*, 31, 112.

Chapter 3

1. Roberts, *Texas, Confederate Military History*, 54; Pettis, "The Confederate Invasion of New Mexico and Arizona," 103; William Davidson in Jerry Thompson, ed., *Civil War in the Southwest: Recollections of the Sibley Brigade* (College Station: Texas A&M University Press, 2001), 4. The standard biography of Sibley is Jerry Don Thompson, *Henry Hopkins Sibley: Confederate General of the West* (Natchitoches: University of Northwestern Louisiana, 1987).
2. Teel, "Sibley's New Mexican Campaign," 700.
3. *O.R.*, L, I, 826, 1071; *O.R.*, IV, 174.
4. James Daniel Richardson, ed., *A Compilation of the Messages and Papers of the Confederacy: Including the Diplomatic Correspondence, 1861–1865* (Nashville, Tenn.: United States Publishing Co., 1906), II, 78; Ronnie C. Tyler, *Santiago Vidaurri and the Southern Confederacy* (Austin: Texas State Historical Association, 1973), 52–53.
5. Tom Green to Nathan Green, 24 September 1861, General Tom Green Collection, Tom Green County Historical Society, West Texas Collection (Angelo State University, San Angelo). Quoted in Curtis W. Milbourn, ed., "'I Have Been Worse Treated than Any Officer': Confederate General Tom Green's Assessment of the New Mexico Campaign," *Southwestern Historical Quarterly*, CV, 2 (October 2001), 325–326; *O.R.*, IV, 168. For an extended treatment of Sibley's attempt at solidifying diplomatic relations with Mexico, see Martin Hardwick Hall, "Colonel James Reily's Diplomatic Missions to Chihuahua and Sonora," *New Mexico Historical Review*, XXXI (July 1956), 232–242.
6. *O.R.*, IV, 167, 172; *O.R.*, L, I, 767.
7. *O.R.*, IV, 174.
8. *O.R.*, IV, 172.
9. OR, L, I, 93, 989, 1042.
10. *O.R.*, L, I, 93, 1118.
11. David B. Gracy II, ed., "New Mexico Campaign Letters of Frank Starr, 1861–1862," *Texas Military History*, IV (1964), 170–171; Walter A. Faulkner, ed., "With Sibley in New Mexico: The Journal of William Henry Smith," *West Texas Historical Association Yearbook*, XXVII (October, 1951), 113; J. L. McLeary, "History of Green's Brigade," in Dudley G. Wooten, ed., *A Comprehensive History of Texas*,

1685 to 1897 (Dallas: William G. Scarff, 1898; rept., Austin: Texas State Historical Association, 1986), volume II, 696.
William Steele, to whom Tom Green referred as "a distinguished dragoon of the old army," was an 1840 graduate of West Point and an experienced officer in antebellum U.S. Army. In addition to the three original regiments of Texas cavalry—the Fourth, under Colonel James Reily; the Fifth, under Colonel Tom Green; and the Seventh, under Colonel William Steele, were later added the First Texas Cavalry, William P. Hardeman, colonel; Second cavalry, George W. Baylor, colonel; Third Cavalry, Joseph Phillips, colonel; Fourth cavalry, Spruce M. Baird, colonel; P. T. Herbert's cavalry battalion, P. T. Herbert, lieutenant-colonel. Oran M. Roberts, *Texas*, Volume X/1 in Clement A. Evans, ed., *Confederate Military History* (Atlanta, Ga.: Confederate Publishing Co., 1899), 54.

12. Gracy, ed., "New Mexico Campaign Letters of Frank Starr," 183–184.
13. Jerry Thompson, ed., *Civil War in the Southwest*, 8; Milbourn, ed., "Tom Green's Assessment of the New Mexico Campaign," 329, 335–336.
14. Thompson, ed., *Civil War in the Southwest*, 7; Hollister, *History of the First Regiment of Colorado Volunteers*, 176; Oscar Haas, trans. and ed., "The Diary of Julius Giesecke, 1861–1862," *Texas Military History* III (Winter 1963), 233; Teel, "Sibley's New Mexican Campaign," 700.
15. Thompson, ed., *Civil War in the Southwest*, 7.
16. Thompson, ed., *Civil War in the Southwest*, 10; Pettis, "The Confederate Invasion of New Mexico and Arizona," 103; McLeary, "History of Green's Brigade," 695–740.
17. Thompson, ed., *Civil War in the Southwest*, 9–11; McLeary, "History of Green's Brigade," 697; Haas, trans. and ed., "The Diary of Julius Giesecke," 229.
18. Faulkner, ed., "With Sibley in New Mexico," 11; Haas, trans. and ed., "The Diary of Julius Giesecke," 230, 231; McLeary, "History of Green's Brigade," 697.
19. Haas, trans. and ed., "The Diary of Julius Giesecke," 232; Thompson, ed., *Civil War in the Southwest*, 14.
20. Pettis, "The Confederate Invasion of New Mexico and Arizona," 103.
21. Hall, ed., "The Taylor Letters," 59; Faulkner, ed., "With Sibley in New Mexico," 124–133; McLeary, "History of Green's Brigade," 695–740.
22. Canby claimed 3,810 men, of whom 1,200 were regulars—five companies of the Fifth, three of the Seventh, and three of the Tenth U.S. Infantry; two companies of the First and five of the Third U.S. Cavalry; and McRae's and Hall's batteries. His volunteer units consisted of Captain Theodore Dodd's independent company of Colorado volunteers, Kit Carson's First, seven companies of the Second, seven companies of the Third, one of the Fourth, and two of the Fifth New Mexico, Graydon's Spy Company, and some and 1,000 hastily collected an unorganized militia in whom he had no confidence. Pettis, "The Confederate Invasion of New Mexico and Arizona," 106; Faulkner, ed., "With Sibley in New Mexico," 126, 134; *O.R.*, IX, 488; Hall, ed., "The Taylor Letters," 59.
23. Faulkner, ed., "With Sibley in New Mexico," 133; Pettis, "The Confederate Invasion of New Mexico and Arizona," 104; Hollister, *History of the First Regiment of Colorado Volunteers*, 163.
24. Hollister, *History of the First Regiment of Colorado Volunteers*, 162–163, 174; Faulkner, ed., "With Sibley in New Mexico," 134; Albert Z. Carr, *The World and William Walker* (New York: Harper & Row, 1963), 215.

Chapter 4

1. Milbourn, ed., "Tom Green's Assessment of the New Mexico Campaign," 329.
2. The First [Fourth] and Second [Fifth] regiments, five companies of the Third [Seventh], five companies of Baylor's regiment, and Captain Trevanian T. Teel's fifteen pieces of artillery. All of Teel's guns were 12-pounder howitzers except four, which were 6-pounder field pieces. Pettis, "The Confederate Invasion of New Mexico and Arizona," 104; Gracy, ed., "New Mexico Campaign Letters of Frank Starr," 171–172, 175–176; Hollister, *History of the First Regiment of Colorado Volunteers*, 174. McLeary, "History of Green's Brigade," 698.
3. Hollister, *History of the First Regiment of Colorado Volunteers*, 174; William Clarke Whitford, *Colorado Volunteers in the Civil War* (Denver: State and Natural History Society, 1906), 57–58.
4. Gracy, ed., "New Mexico Campaign Letters of Frank Starr," 172; Hollister, *History of the First Regiment of Colorado Volunteers*, 174; McLeary, "History of Green's Brigade," 695–740; Faulkner, ed., "With Sibley in New Mexico," 135; F. S. Wade, "The Battle of Valverde," *Confederate Veteran*, XXIX (April 1821), 137–138; Haas, trans. and ed., "The Diary of Julius Giesecke," 233; Pettis, "The Confederate Invasion of New Mexico and Arizona," 104–105.
5. Pettis, "The Confederate Invasion of New Mexico and Arizona," II, 105; Hollister, *Colorado Volunteers in New Mexico*, 155–156; *O.R.*, IX, 496. For a full treatment of Graydon's life and exploits, see Jerry D. Thompson, *Desert Tiger: Captain Paddy Graydon and the Civil War in the Far Southwest* (El Paso: Texas Western Press, 1992).
6. Pettis, "The Confederate Invasion of New Mexico and Arizona," 105–106; Thompson. *Desert Tiger*, 35.
7. Anderson, "Canby's Services in the New Mexican Campaign," 698–699.
8. *O.R.*, IV, 131–132; McLeary, "History of Green's Brigade," 698.
9. Pettis, "The Confederate Invasion of New Mexico and Arizona," 106–107; Joseph McClellan Bell in Theophilus Francis Rodenbough, comp., *From Everglade to Cañon with the Second Dragoons* (New York: Van Nostrand, 1875), 239.
10. Thomas Benton Collins, "A Texan's Account of the Battle of Valverde," *Panhandle Plains Historical Review*, XXXVI (1964), 34.
11. Gracy, ed., "New Mexico Campaign Letters of Frank Starr," 172; Milbourn, ed., "Tom Green's Assessment of the New Mexico Campaign," 329; Roberts, *Texas*, 150–151. The standard monograph on this battle, fought on 21 February 1862, is John Taylor, *Bloody Valverde: A Civil War Battle on the Rio Grande, February 21, 1862* (Albuquerque: University of New Mexico Press, 1995).
12. Wade, "The Battle of Valverde," 137–138; Oscar Haas, trans. and ed., "The Diary of Julius Giesecke, 235; Pettis, "The Confederate Invasion of New Mexico and Arizona," 107

    The Confederates estimated Canby's command at between 3,810 and 7,000 effective men, "all well-armed and equipped." This force consisted of 1,500 regulars: five companies of the Fifth Infantry, three companies of the Seventh Infantry, and three companies of the Tenth Infantry, plus two companies of the First and five of the Third Cavalry and Captain Alexander McRae's and Captain Robert H. Hall's batteries. In addition, Canby commanded one company of Colorado volunteers, the First New Mexico Infantry, seven companies of the Second New Mexico Infantry, seven companies of the Third New Mexico Infantry, one company of the Fourth New Mexico Infantry, two companies of the Fifth New Mexico Infantry, Graydon's Spy

Company, and some unorganized militia. Pettis, "The Confederate Invasion of New Mexico and Arizona," 106–107; McLeary, "History of Green's Brigade," 695–740.

13. Milbourn, ed., "Tom Green's Assessment of the New Mexico Campaign," 329; Pettis, "The Confederate Invasion of New Mexico and Arizona," 108–109.
14. Don E. Alberts, ed., *Rebels on the Rio Grande: The Civil War Journal of A. B. Peticolas* (Albuquerque: University of New Mexico Press, 1984), 42.
15. Sibley seems to have suffered from a mysterious chronic illness and, according to his best biographer, "for several years his custom had been to resort to alcohol" to relieve his discomfort. Thompson, *Sibley*, 252; Alberts, ed., *Rebels on the Rio Grande*, 41–42.
16. Teel had four 6-pounder field guns and eleven 12-pounder mountain howitzers of shorter range and therefore limited use.
17. Alberts, ed., *Rebels on the Rio Grande*, 42–43; Gracy, ed., "New Mexico Campaign Letters of Frank Starr," 172.
18. *O.R.*, IX, 513–514; Alberts, ed., *Rebels on the Rio Grande*, 45.
19. Alberts, ed., *Rebels on the Rio Grande*, 44.
20. Thompson, ed., *Civil War in the Southwest*, 32; Gracy, ed., "New Mexico Campaign Letters of Frank Starr," 173–174; Alberts, ed., *Rebels on the Rio Grande*, 45. Exact figures cannot be determined. Sibley probably had about 2,000 men at Valverde. Canby had a total of 3,800 men at Fort Craig. His field force included only about 1,200 regulars, with the balance being made up of volunteers and militiaman without significant experience or adequate training. The Federal force had eight guns: Captain Robert H. Hall's battery of two 24-pounder howitzers; Captain Alexander McRae's battery of one 12-pounder mountain howitzer, two 12-pounder field howitzers, and three 6-pounder field guns. *O.R.*, IX, 496, 502–503; Richard K. McMaster and George Ruhlen, "The Guns of Val Verde," *Password*, V (January 1980), 26–28; Alberts, *Rebels on the Rio Grande*, 49.
21. Tom Green reported that this movement came at about 4:30 PM. The confusion of combat, the fading of memory, and the lack of standard time conspire to render virtually useless all reported times in reconstructing a chronology of events on any battlefield, and indeed, differing accounts often conflict on dates of certain events. As Captain Hollister remarked regarding Valverde, "It is impossible to give a reliable statement of the affair as everyone tells a different story." Milbourn, ed., "Tom Green's Assessment of the New Mexico Campaign," 331–332; Anderson, "Canby's Services in the New Mexican Campaign," 698–699; Wade, "The Battle of Valverde," 137–138; Tate, ed., "A Johnny Reb and in Sibley's New Mexico Campaign," 31; Bell in Rodenbough, comp., *From Everglade to Cañon*, 239; Hollister, *History of the First Colorado Volunteers*, 86; Alberts, ed., *Rebels on the Rio Grande*, 48; Pettis, "The Confederate Invasion of New Mexico and Arizona," 106–108.
22. Milbourn, ed., "Tom Green's Assessment of the New Mexico Campaign," 329.
23. F. S. Wade later remembered the time of the charge as about 2:00 PM; Lang, himself, said 5:00. Hollister, *History of the First Regiment of Colorado Volunteers*, 176–177; Wade, "The Battle of Valverde," 137–138; Bell, "The Campaign of New Mexico," 62; Ickis Diary, entry for February 21, 1862; Alberts, ed., *Rebels on the Rio Grande*, 53; Thomas W. Cutrer, ed., "'My Wild Hunt after Indians': The Journal of Willis L. Lang, First Lieutenant, Waco Rangers, 23 April–7 September 1860," *Military History of the Southwest*, XXII, 1 (Spring 1991), 20–58.
24. Milbourn, ed., "Tom Green's Assessment of the New Mexico Campaign," 329; *Confederate Military History*, 151; A. W. Evans, "Canby at Valverde," 699–701.

25. Milbourn, ed., "Tom Green's Assessment of the New Mexico Campaign," 331–332; Wade, "The Battle of Valverde," 137–138; McLeary, "History of Green's Brigade," 695–740; Gracy, ed., "New Mexico Campaign Letters of Frank Starr," 174; Alberts, ed., *Rebels on the Rio Grande*, 48.
26. *O.R.*, IX, 519; Milbourn, ed., "Tom Green's Assessment of the New Mexico Campaign," 330–332; Bell, in Rodenbough, comp., *From Everglade to Cañon*, 239–241; Hollister, *History of the First Regiment of Colorado Volunteers*, 179–180; Alberts, ed., *Rebels on the Rio Grande*, 48.
27. Tate, ed., "A Johnny Reb and in Sibley's New Mexico Campaign," 24.
28. Gracy, ed., "New Mexico Campaign Letters of Frank Starr," 174; Wade, "Battle of Val Verde," 137–138; Tate, ed., "A Johnny Reb and in Sibley's New Mexico Campaign," 24; H. C. Wright, "Reminiscences of H. C. Wright of Austin," Barker Texas History Center, University of Texas, Austin, Texas.
29. Wright, "Reminiscences of H. C. Wright; Roberts, *Texas*, 151.
30. Gracy, ed., "New Mexico Campaign Letters of Frank Starr," 174; Tate, ed., "A Johnny Reb and in Sibley's New Mexico Campaign," 20–33; Alberts, ed., *Rebels on the Rio Grande*, 48; Roberts, *Texas*, 151; Wade, "The Battle of Valverde," 137–138; A. W. Evans, "Canby at Valverde," 699-700; *O.R.*, IX, 493.
31. *O.R.*, IX, 491; McLeary, "History of Green's Brigade," 699; Bell in Rodenbough, comp., *From Everglade to Cañon*, 24–241; Alberts, ed., *Rebels on the Rio Grande*, 48; Pettis, "The Confederate Invasion of New Mexico and Arizona," 107–109; Milbourn, ed., "Tom Green's Assessment of the New Mexico Campaign," 331; Alberts, ed., *Rebels on the Rio Grande*, 48; Gracy, ed., "New Mexico Campaign Letters of Frank Starr," 175.
    Numerous versions of the deaths of Lockridge and McRea were reported. Both William Clarke Whitford in *Colorado Volunteers and the Civil War*, 65, and George H. Pettis, "The Confederate Invasion of New Mexico and Arizona," 108, claimed that Lockridge, standing at the muzzle of the guns, demanded McRae's surrender, which was refused. Then the two men aimed their pistols, fired, and killed each other. Teel, cited in a footnote to Pettis's article on page 108, stated that no such duel took place. In response to Lockridge's claim to the cannon, McCrae is supposed to have shouted to his men, "shoot the son of a bitch." Alberts, ed., *Rebels on the Rio Grande*, 48.
32. Pettis, "The Confederate Invasion of New Mexico and Arizona," 107–108; Bell in Rodenbough, comp., *From Everglade to Cañon*, 240–241; Hollister, *History of the First Regiment of Colorado Volunteers*, 181.
33. John William Ellis to Winfield S. Fletcher, Adjutant General, Territory of New Mexico, 17 May 1892, in J. Robert Feynn, ed., "A Soldier in New Mexico, 1860–1865," *El Palicio*, LXV (August 1958), 143–144.
34. Roberts, *Texas*, 151; Gracy, ed., "New Mexico Campaign Letters of Frank Starr," 174; Pettis, "The Confederate Invasion of New Mexico and Arizona," 107–109; *O.R.*, IX, 520; Milbourn, ed., "Tom Green's Assessment of the New Mexico Campaign," 331.
35. Bell, in Rodenbough, comp., *From Everglade to Cañon*, 240–241; Hollister, *History of the First Regiment of Colorado Volunteers*, 182; Tate, ed., "A Johnny Reb and in Sibley's New Mexico Campaign," 24; Collins, "A Texan's Account of the Battle of Valverde," 35; McLeary, "History of Green's Brigade," 695–740.
36. Milbourn, ed., "Tom Green's Assessment of the New Mexico Campaign," 329; Roberts, *Texas*, 150–151; McLeary, "History of Green's Brigade," 699–700.
37. *O.R.*, IX, 493, 521, 647; Alberts, ed., *Rebels on the Rio Grande*, 49; Pettis, "The Confederate Invasion of New Mexico and Arizona," 108; Roberts, *Texas*, 152–154.

38. Tate, ed., "A Johnny Reb and in Sibley's New Mexico Campaign," 24–25; McLeary, "History of Green's Brigade," 699–700; Gracy, ed., "New Mexico Campaign Letters of Frank Starr," 175; Alberts, ed., *Rebels on the Rio Grande*, 51–52.
39. John William Ellis to Winfield S. Fletcher, Adjutant General, Territory of New Mexico, 17 May 1892, in J. Robert Feynn, ed., "A Soldier in New Mexico, 1860–1865," *El Palicio*, LXV (August 1958), 143–144; Pettis, "The Confederate Invasion of New Mexico and Arizona," 108.
40. Quoted in Hall, *Sibley's New Mexico Campaign*, 57; Alberts, ed., *Rebels on the Rio Grande*, 50; Gracy, ed., "New Mexico Campaign Letters of Frank Starr," 175–176.
41. Canby to adjutant general, 22 February 1862, *O.R.*, IV?, 169?; McLeary, "History of Green's Brigade," 695–740; Anderson, "Canby's Services in the New Mexican Campaign," 698–699; A. W. Evans, "Canby at Valverde," 700; Hollister, *History of the First Regiment of Colorado Volunteers*, 184.
42. Tate, ed., "A Johnny Reb and in Sibley's New Mexico Campaign," 28; Martin Hardwick Hall, ed., "An Appraisal of the 1862 New Mexico Campaign: A Confederate Officer's Letter to Natchitoches," *New Mexico Historical Review*, LI, 4, (October 1976), 332; Wade, "The Battle of Valverde," 137–138.

Chapter 5

1. Gracy, ed., "New Mexico Campaign Letters of Frank Starr," 175–176; Alberts, ed., *Rebels on the Rio Grande*, 52; Haas, trans. and ed., "The Diary of Julius Giesecke," 235; Hall, ed., "An Appraisal of the 1862 New Mexico Campaign," 332.
2. Whitford, *Colorado Volunteers*, 78; Alberts, ed., *Rebels on the Rio Grande*, 59.
3. Alberts, ed., *Rebels on the Rio Grande*, 59; Hall, ed., "An Appraisal of the 1862 New Mexico Campaign," 332.
4. Alberts, ed., *Rebels on the Rio Grande*, 101; McLeary, "History of Green's Brigade," 695–740; Pettis, "The Confederate Invasion of New Mexico and Arizona," 108; Haas, trans. and ed., "The Diary of Julius Giesecke," 236–237.
5. McLeary, "History of Green's Brigade," 103.
6. *O.R.*, L, 942.
7. C. L. Sonnichsen, *The Mescalero Apaches* (Norman: University of Oklahoma Press, 1958), 103.
8. Thompson, ed., *From Desert to Bayou*, 35; E. E. Townsend, "The Mays Massacre," *West Texas Historical and Scientific Society Public Bulletin*, 48 (1933), 29–43; *El Paso Herald*, 24 June 1905, 13.
9. In January 1863, however, Baylor was elected to the House of Representatives in the Second Confederate Congress. J. P. Benjamin to Jefferson Davis, Earl Schenck Miers, ed., *A Rebel War Clerk's Diary* (New York: Sagamore Press, 1958), 117–118; *O.R.*, Series IV, Volume I, 791–792; Thompson, ed., *From Desert to Bayou*, 31; Martin Hardwick Hall, "The Baylor-Kelley Fight: A Civil War Incident in Old Mesilla," *Password*, July 1960.
10. Connelly to Seward, 11 March 1862, *O.R.*, IX, 645.
11. Alberts, ed., *Rebels on the Rio Grande*, 54; *O.R.*, IX, 605.
12. Haas, trans. and ed., "The Diary of Julius Giesecke," 235; McLeary, "History of Green's Brigade," 695–740; Tate, ed., "A Johnny Reb and in Sibley's New Mexico Campaign," 28; Faulkner, ed., "With Sibley in New Mexico," 137; Haas, trans. and ed., "The Diary of Julius Giesecke," 236.
13. Peticolas was correct when he wrote that "I don't expect we will ever take horses and up to mount the regiment again," and the dismounted men never received

compensation for the horses they willingly turned over to their comrades. Noel, *A Campaign from Santa Fe to the Mississippi*, 31; Alberts, ed., *Rebels on the Rio Grande*, 55–56, 61.

14. Faulkner, ed., "With Sibley in New Mexico," 137.
15. Faulkner, ed., "With Sibley in New Mexico," 137; Haas, trans. and ed., "The Diary of Julius Giesecke," 236; Alberts, ed., *Rebels on the Rio Grande*, 63.
16. J. H. McLeary, "History of Green's Brigade," 700; Alberts, ed., *Rebels on the Rio Grande*, 61
17. *O.R.*, IX, 649; Hollister, *History of the First Regiment of Colorado Volunteers*, 71–72. According to William Clarke Whitford, the regiment received orders to march to New Mexico on February 10 but did not depart until the twenty-second, the day after the battle of Valverde. William Clarke Whitford, *Colorado Volunteers in the Civil War* (Denver: State Historical and Natural History Society, 1906), 45, 47, 75.
18. Hollister, *History of the First Regiment of Colorado Volunteers*, 71–75.
19. Hollister, *History of the First Colorado*, 75–78.
20. Hollister, *History of the First Colorado Volunteers*, 82–83; Chris Emmett, *Fort Union and the Winning of the Southwest* (Norman: University of Oklahoma Press, 1965).
21. Hollister, *History of the First Colorado Volunteers*, 166; Pettis, "The Confederate Invasion of New Mexico and Arizona" 108.
22. Hollister, *History of the First Colorado Volunteers*, 87.
23. Pettis, "The Confederate Invasion of New Mexico and Arizona" 109; Hollister, *Colorado Volunteers in New Mexico*, 92–93.
24. Gracy, ed., "New Mexico Campaign Letters of Frank Starr," 176.
25. Faulkner, ed., "With Sibley in New Mexico," 138; Hollister, *Colorado Volunteers in New Mexico*, 93–97.
26. Unknown Union diarist, quoted in Hollister, *Colorado Volunteers in New Mexico*, 97–98.
27. The standard histories of the battles of Apache Pass and Glorieta are Don E. Alberts, *The Battle of Glorieta: Union Victory in the West* (College Station: Texas A&M University Press, 1998) and Thomas S. Edrington and John Taylor, *The Battle of Glorieta Pass: A Gettysburg in the West, March 26–28, 1862* (Albuquerque: University of New Mexico Press, 1998). The only full-length biography of the Federal commander at Apache Canyon is Reginald S. Craig, *The Fighting Parson: The Biography of Colonel John M. Chivington* (Los Angeles: Westernlore Press, 1959).
28. Hollister, *Colorado Volunteers in New Mexico*, 99–104.
29. Hollister says that Chivington withdrew all the way to Kozlowski's, there being only one well at Pigeon's Ranch from which to water their stock. *O.R.*, IX, 530–531; Alberts, ed., *Rebels on the Rio Grande*, 76; Hollister, *Colorado Volunteers in New Mexico*, 104–105, 109.
30. Alberts, ed., *Rebels on the Rio Grande*, 75–76; Haas, trans. and ed., "The Diary of Julius Giesecke," 237.
31. Alberts, ed., *Rebels on the Rio Grande*, 76–77; Haas, trans. and ed., "The Diary of Julius Giesecke," 237.
32. Alberts, ed., *Rebels on the Rio Grande*, 77.
33. *O.R.*, IX: 533–535, 538–539, 541–542; Haas, trans. and ed., "The Diary of Julius Giesecke," 237; Hollister, *Colorado Volunteers in New Mexico*, 109–110.
34. Hollister, *Colorado Volunteers in New Mexico*, 109–110.
35. Pettis, "The Confederate Invasion of New Mexico and Arizona" 109.

36. Hollister, *Colorado Volunteers in New Mexico*, 111.
37. Scurry's report, *O.R.*, IX, 544. Alberts, ed., *Rebels on the Rio Grande*, 79; Roberts, *Texas*, 154.
38. Hollister, *Colorado Volunteers in New Mexico*, 111–112; *O.R.*, IX, 542-544; Alberts, ed., *Rebels on the Rio Grande*, 79.
39. Hollister, *Colorado Volunteers in New Mexico*, 112–113.
40. *O.R.*, IX, 536, 539–540; Alberts, ed., *Rebels on the Rio Grande*, 79–81; Hollister, *Colorado Volunteers in New Mexico*, 113, 115.
41. Hollister, *Colorado Volunteers in New Mexico*, 115.
42. Alberts, ed., *Rebels on the Rio Grande*, 84; Hollister, *Colorado Volunteers in New Mexico*, 115.
43. *O.R.*, IX, 538–539, 544; Alberts, ed., *Rebels on the Rio Grande*, 85; Pettis, "The Confederate Invasion of New Mexico and Arizona," 108; Hollister, *Colorado Volunteers in New Mexico*, 115–116.
44. Alberts, ed., *Rebels on the Rio Grande*, 86; Hollister, *Colorado Volunteers in New Mexico*, 116, 118, 134; *O.R.*, IX, 535, 537–538, 545.
45. Hollister, *Colorado Volunteers in New Mexico*, 117; Haas, trans. and ed., "The Diary of Julius Giesecke," 237.
46. Alberts, ed., *Rebels on the Rio Grande*, 86; Haas, trans. and ed., "The Diary of Julius Giesecke," 237; McLeary, "History of Green's Brigade," 703; J. Robert Feynn, ed., "A Soldier in New Mexico, 1860–1865," *El Palicio,* LXV (August 1958), 143–144.
47. Slough was honorably discharged from U.S. service on April 12, 1862 but was subsequently reinstated as a brigadier general of volunteers. Although Hollister characterized Slough as "a man of undoubted ability and bravery," he complained that his "personal contact with his men was never of a kind to make him beloved. He wanted tact and policy." Pettis, "The Confederate Invasion of New Mexico and Arizona," 109; *O.R.*, IX, 537–538, 540 544; Hollister, *Colorado Volunteers in New Mexico*, 121, 127, 138–139; Arthur A. Wright, "Why Did Colonel Slough Resign?" and "Colonel John P. Slough," *The Colorado Magazine*, XXXIX (April 1962), 89–106.
48. Headquarters, Advance Division, Army of New Mexico; Canyon Glorieta, March 29, 1862, General Order Number 4, quoted in Alberts, ed., *Rebels on the Rio Grande*, 90.

Chapter 6

1. The "Colorados," as well, helped themselves to citizens' property. At Fort Union on the night of March 21, Hollister admitted, "the boys broke into the sutler's cellar and gobbled a lot of whiskey, wine, canned fruit, oysters, etc." Haas, trans. and ed., "The Diary of Julius Giesecke," 237; Faulkner, ed., "With Sibley in New Mexico," 139; Alberts, ed., *Rebels on the Rio Grande*, 91–92; Hollister, *History of the First Colorado Volunteers*, 88.
2. *O.R.*, IX, 549–550, 552; Hollister, *Boldly they Rode*, 78–89; Alberts, ed., *Rebels on the Rio Grande*, 126–128; Pettis, "Confederate Invasion of New Mexico," 109–110; Haas, trans. and ed., "The Diary of Julius Giesecke, 238.
3. Alberts, ed., *Rebels on the Rio Grande* 97–98; Hollister, *Colorado Volunteers in New Mexico*, 134.
4. *O.R.*, IX, 549–551; Jacob Downing and John D. Allen, "On the Gory Field of Glorieta Heights," *Santa Fe New Mexican*, 7 August 1906; Alberts, ed., *Rebels on the Rio Grande*, 96.
5. McLeary, "History of Green's Brigade." 703–704.

6. Anderson, "Canby's Services in the New Mexican Campaign," 698–699; Gracy, ed., "New Mexico Campaign Letters of Frank Starr," 178–180.
7. Alberts, ed., *Rebels on the Rio Grande*, 98–101; Gracy, ed., "New Mexico Campaign Letters of Frank Starr," 178–179; Haas, trans. and editor, "The Diary of Julius Giesecke," 238; Hall, ed., "An Appraisal of the 1862 New Mexico Campaign," 331; McLeary, "History of Green's Brigade," 704; John Henry Brown, *Indian Wars and Pioneers of Texas* (Austin: L. E. Daniel, 1896), 398.
8. *O.R.*, IX, 550; Alberts, ed., *Rebels on the Rio Grande*, 97; Hollister, *Colorado Volunteers in New Mexico*, 135; Pettis, "The Confederate Invasion of New Mexico and Arizona," 109–110; Haas, trans. and ed., "The Diary of Julius Giesecke, 238.
9. Gracy, ed., "New Mexico Campaign Letters of Frank Starr," 178–179; Alberts, ed., *Rebels on the Rio Grande*, 101.
10. McLeary, "History of Green's Brigade," 704; Pettis, "The Confederate Invasion of New Mexico and Arizona," 109–110; Haas, trans. and ed., "The Diary of Julius Giesecke, 238; Alberts, ed., *Rebels on the Rio Grande*, 101–102; *O.R.*, IX, 510–511; Noel, *History of the Sibley Brigade*, 26–27.
11. Milbourn, ed., "Assessment of the New Mexico Campaign," 334; *O.R.*, IX, 551, 665; J. M. Bell, "The Campaign of New Mexico, 1862," *War Papers Read Before the Commandry of the State of Wisconsin, Military Order of the Loyal Legion of the United States*. (Milwaukee: Burdick, Armitage and Allen, 1891), I: 67–68; Alberts, ed., *Rebels on the Rio Grande*, 102–107.
12. Hollister, *Colorado Volunteers in New Mexico*, 146–148.
13. Hollister, *Colorado Volunteers in New Mexico*, 150–152.
14. Alberts, ed., *Rebels on the Rio Grande*, 102–107; *O.R.*, IX, 551; Hollister, *Colorado Volunteers in New Mexico*, 144, 146–147.
15. Hollister, *Colorado Volunteers in New Mexico*, 151; *O.R.*, IX, 551.
16. A Private of the Regiment, *The March of the First: Being a History of the Organization, Marches, Battles and Services of the First Regiment, of Colorado Volunteers, the Names of the Members of the Regiment, a List of Officers and Promotions, with a Full List of Killed, Dead and Wounded by a Private of the Regiment* (Denver, C.T.: Thomas Gibson & Co., 1863), 19–20; Hollister, *Colorado Volunteers in New Mexico*, 152–153; Alberts, ed., *Rebels on the Rio Grande*, 106; Don E. Alberts, "The Battle of Peralta," *New Mexico Historical Review* 58 (October 1983), 369–379; *O.R.*, IX, 510, 551; Bell, "The Campaign in New Mexico," 69–70.
17. McLeary, "History of Green's Brigade," 704–705; Alberts, ed., *Rebels on the Rio Grande*, 97, 99–101; Hollister, *Colorado Volunteers in New Mexico*, 158.
18. Hollister, *Colorado Volunteers in New Mexico*, 154–155.
19. Hollister, *Colorado Volunteers in New Mexico*, 142–143.
20. Haas, trans. and ed., "The Diary of Julius Giesecke," 238; Hollister, *Colorado Volunteers in New Mexico*, 152.
21. Alberts, ed., *Rebels on the Rio Grande*, 108.
22. Hollister, *Colorado Volunteers in New Mexico*, 158–159.
23. Alberts, ed., *Rebels on the Rio Grande*, 108–109.
24. Gracy, ed., "New Mexico Campaign Letters of Frank Starr," 180.
25. Alberts, ed., *Rebels on the Rio Grande*, 108–109.
26. An unknown number of guns were buried in Santa Fe, and eight mountain howitzers were buried near the Albuquerque plaza. In 1889, twenty-seven years afterward, Trevanian T. Teel relocated the howitzers, two of which were presented to the

Albuquerque Museum. Gracy, ed., "Starr Campaign Letters," 179–180; Howard Bryan, "The Man Who Buried the Cannons," *New Mexico Magazine*, XL (January, 1962), 15; Alberts, ed., *Rebels on the Rio Grande*, 141.

27. Alberts, ed., *Rebels on the Rio Grande*, 94; McLeary, "History of Green's Brigade," 705; Gracy, ed., "New Mexico Campaign Letters of Frank Starr," 178–181; Haas, trans. and ed., "The Diary of Julius Giesecke," 238.
28. "This water we found extremely unpalatable and salty," Peticloas agreed," and the coffee made from it was hardly fit to drink atall, and as we had nothing but coffee and bread, we had pretty hard fare." Alberts, ed., *Rebels on the Rio Grande*, 109; Haas, trans. and ed., "The Diary of Julius Giesecke," 238; Hollister, *Colorado Volunteers in New Mexico*, 160–163; Pettis, "The Confederate Invasion of New Mexico and Arizona" 111.
29. Alberts, ed., *Rebels on the Rio Grande*, 112–113.
30. *O.R.*, IX, 671–672; Alberts, ed., *Rebels on the Rio Grande*, 113.
31. Gracy, ed., "Starr Campaign Letters," 178, 181; Alberts, ed., *Rebels on the Rio Grande*, 113.
32. *O.R.*, IX, 571–572; Alberts, ed., *Rebels on the Rio Grande*, 112; Hall, ed., "An Appraisal of the 1862 New Mexico Campaign," 331.
33. Haas, trans. and ed., "The Diary of Julius Giesecke," 238–239; Holister, *Colorado Volunteers in New Mexico*, 168–169.
34. Alberts, ed., *Rebels on the Rio Grande*, 215; Haas, trans. and ed., "The Diary of Julius Giesecke," 239.
35. Alberts, ed., *Rebels on the Rio Grande*, 215; Haas, trans. and ed., "The Diary of Julius Giesecke," 239; Gracy, ed., "New Mexico Campaign Letters of Frank Starr," 178. For Sibley's report on the New Mexico campaign, see Sibley to Cooper, 4 May 1862, Fort Bliss, *O.R.*, IX, 506–512.
36. *O.R.*, IX, 672; Noel, *Campaign from Santa Fe*, 28; Pettis, "The Confederate Invasion of New Mexico and Arizona" 110.
37. Hollister, *Colorado Volunteers in New Mexico*, 168–169, 185–186, 195; Pettis, "The Confederate Invasion of New Mexico and Arizona" 110.
38. Darlis A. Miller, *The California Column in New Mexico* (Albuquerque: University of New Mexico Press, 1982), 9.
39. *O.R.*, IX, 707–708; L. Boyd Finch, "Sherod Hunter and the Confederates in Arizona," *Journal of Arizona History*, X (fall 1982), 203; *Sacramento Union*, 23 May 1862; Richard H. Orton, *California Men in the War of the Rebellion, 1861 to 1867* (Sacramento: California Adjutant General's Office, 1890), 69, 90, 98, 107, 109, 120; George H. Pettis to Annie (wife), 30 April 1862, George H. Pettis Papers, Western American Collection, Beinecke Library, Yale, New Haven, Connecticut; George Henry Pettis, *The California Column: It's Campaigns and Services in New Mexico, Arizona and Texas during the Civil War* (Santa Fe: Historical Society of New Mexico, 1908), 9; Henry P. Walker, ed., "Soldier in the California Column: The Diary of John W. Teal," *Arizona and the West*, XIII, 1 (spring 1971), 45.
40. Haas, trans. and ed., "The Diary of Julius Giesecke," 239; Alberts, ed., *Rebels on the Rio Grande*, 117.
41. Gracy, ed., "Starr Campaign Letters," 178, 182.
42. Noel, *A Campaign from Santa Fe to the Mississippi*, 28, 51; Teel, "Sibley's New Mexican Campaign," 700.
43. Alberts, ed., *Rebels on the Rio Grande*, 123; Haas, trans. and ed., "The Diary of Julius Giesecke," 239.

44. Haas, trans. and ed., "The Diary of Julius Giesecke," 239; Mother Magdalen Hayden to "Sister," quoted in Alberts, ed., *Rebels on the Rio Grande*, 87–88; Alberts, ed., *Rebels on the Rio Grande*, 128; Gracy, ed., "New Mexico Campaign Letters of Frank Starr," 194.
45. Alberts, ed., *Rebels on the Rio Grande*, 129.
46. Sibley quoted in Noel, *Campaign from Santa Fe*, 39; Gracy, ed., "New Mexico Campaign Letters of Frank Starr," 187.
47. Alberts, ed., *Rebels on the Rio Grande*, 152; Gracy, ed., "New Mexico Campaign Letters of Frank Starr," 185; Hall, ed., "An Appraisal of the 1862 New Mexico Campaign," 330–331.
48. Hall, ed., "An Appraisal of the 1862 New Mexico Campaign," 330; Alberts, ed., *Rebels on the Rio Grande*, 143.
49. Hall, ed., "An Appraisal of the 1862 New Mexico Campaign," 331; Gracy, ed., "New Mexico Campaign Letters of Frank Starr," 186–187; Alberts, ed., *Rebels on the Rio Grande*, 137.
50. Haas, trans. and ed., "The Diary of Julius Giesecke," 239–242; Alberts, ed., *Rebels on the Rio Grande*, 143–152.
51. Hollister, *History of the First Regiment of Colorado Volunteers*, 197; J. Robert Seynn, ed., "A Soldier in New Mexico, 1860–1865," *El Palicio*, LXV (August 1958), 144; Miller, *The California Column in New Mexico*, 13–15; *O.R.*, IX, 678–680, 686–688.
52. Haas, trans. and ed., "The Diary of Julius Giesecke," 242; McLeary, "History of Green's Brigade," 706; Gracy, ed., "New Mexico Campaign Letters of Frank Starr," 178, 188.
53. Haas, trans. and ed., "The Diary of Julius Giesecke," 239; Hall, *Confederate Army of New Mexico*, 202–203.
54. Gracy, ed., "New Mexico Campaign Letters of Frank Starr," 177–178; Capt. J. B. McCown, Company C, Fifth Texas, to editor, *Countryman*, 6 May, 1862, in the *Belleville Countryman*, 7 June 1862, quoted in Alberts, ed., *Rebels on the Rio Grande*, 153.
55. Gracy, ed., "New Mexico Campaign Letters of Frank Starr," 178; Hall, ed., "An Appraisal of the 1862 New Mexico Campaign," 332.
56. Gracy, ed., "New Mexico Campaign Letters of Frank Starr," 186–187.
57. Hall, ed., "An Appraisal of the 1862 New Mexico Campaign," 331; Gracy, ed., "New Mexico Campaign Letters of Frank Starr," 178; "First Congress—Second Session," *Southern Historical Society Papers*, 21–22.
58. *O.R.*, IX, 666.
59. *The March of the First*, 242–243.
60. *O.R.*, L, II, 700–701.
61. Anderson, "Canby's Services in the New Mexican Campaign," 698; Anderson, "Canby's Services in the New Mexican Campaign," 698.

Bibliography

Primary and Contemporary Sources

Books

A Private of the Regiment. *The March of the First: Being a History of the Organization, Marches, Battles and Services of the First Regiment, of Colorado Volunteers, the Names of the Members of the Regiment, a List of Officers and Promotions, with a Full List of Killed, Dead and Wounded by* a Private of the Regiment. Denver, CT: Thomas Gibson & Co., 1863.

Albert, James A. *Albert's New Mexico Report, 1846–1847.* Albuquerque: Horne and Wallace, 1962.

Alberts, Don E., ed., *Rebels on the Rio Grande: The Civil War Journal of the A. B. Peticolas.* Albuquerque: University of New Mexico Press, 1984.

Baylor, George Wythe. *Into the Far, Wild Country: True Tales of the Old Southwest,* edited, Jerry Thompson. El Paso: Texas Western Press, 1996.

Baylor, George Wythe. *John Robert Baylor.* Odie B. Faulk, ed., Tucson: Arizona Pioneers Historical Society, 1966.

Carmony, Neil B., ed. *The Civil War in Apacheland: Sergeant George Hand's Diary: California, Arizona, West Texas, New Mexico, 1861–1864.* Silver City, NM: High-Lonesome Books, 1996.

D'Hamel, Enrique B. *The Adventures of a Tenderfoot: History of the 2nd Regt. Mounted Rifles and Co. G, 33rd Regt. and Capt. Coopwood's Spy Co and 2nd Texas in Texas and New Mexico.* Waco, TX: W. M. Morrison Books, 1914.

Faulkner, Walter A. ed. "With Sibley in New Mexico: The Journal of William Henry Smith," *West Texas Historical Association Yearbook,* XXVII (October, 1951), 111–142.

Gracy, David B., II, ed. "New Mexico Campaign Letters of Frank Starr, 1861–1862," *Texas Military History,* IV (1964), 169–188.

Hollister, Ovando J. *History of the First Regiment of Colorado Volunteers.* Denver: Thomas Gibson and Co., 1863; reprinted as Richard Harwell, ed., *Colorado Volunteers in New Mexico, 1862.* Chicago: The Lakeside Press, 1962.

Lane, Lydia Spencer. *I Married a Soldier or Old Days in the Old Army.* Albuquerque: Horn and Wallace, 1964.

McCall, George Archibald. *New Mexico in 1850: A Military View.* Robert W. Frazer, ed., Norman: University of Oklahoma Press, 1968.

McKee, James Cooper. *Narrative of the Surrender of a Command of the U.S. Forces at Fort Fillmore New Mexico in July, A.D. 1861, with Related Reports by John R. Baylor, C.S.A., and Others.* Boston, 1886; Houston: Stagecoach Press, 1960.

Mumey, Nolie, ed. *Bloody Trails along the Rio Grande: A Day-By-Day Diary of Alonzo Ferdinand Ickis 1836–1917: A Soldier and His Activities with Company B; the First Volunteer Regiment to Leave the Territory of Colorado for the Civil War: Their Participation in the Battle of Valverede, New Mexico.* Denver: Old West Publishing Co., 1958.

Orton, Richard H., comp. *California Men in the War of the Rebellion, 1861 to 1867.* Sacramento: California Adjutant General's Office, 1890.

Thompson, Jerry, ed. *Civil War in the Southwest: Recollections of the Sibley Brigade.* College Station: Texas A&M University Press, 2001.

Thompson, Jerry D., ed. *From Desert to Bayou: The Civil War Journal and Sketches of Morgan Wolfe Merrick.* El Paso: Texas Western Press., 1991.

Thompson, Jerry D., ed. *New Mexico Territory during the Civil War: Wallen and Evans Inspection Reports, 1862–1863.* Albuquerque: University of New Mexico Press, 2008.

Thompson, Jerry D., ed. *Westward the Texans: The Civil War Journal of Private William Randolph Howell.* El Paso: Texas Western Press, 1990.

Whitford, William Clarke. *Colorado Volunteers in the Civil War, The New Mexico Campaign in 1862.* Colorado State Historical and Natural History Society, 1906, Republished, Pruett Press, Boulder, CO, 1963.

Whitlock, Flint. *Distant Bugles, Distant Drums: The Union Response to the Confederate Invasion of New Mexico.* Boulder: University Press of Colorado, 2006.

Williams, Mrs. Ellen. *Three Years and a Half in the Army, History of the Second Colorados.* New York: Fowler & Wells Company, 1885.

Wilson, John P., ed. *When the Texans Came: Missing Records from the Civil; War in the Southwest,* 1861–1862. Albuquerque: University of New Mexico Press, 2001.

Wilson, John P., and Jerry Thompson, eds. *The Civil War in West Texas and New Mexico: The Lost Letterbook of Brigadier General Henry Hopkins Sibley.* College Station: Texas A&M University Press, 2001.

Articles

Anderson, Hattie M., ed. "With the Confederates in New Mexico during the Civil War—Memoirs of Hank Smith." *Panhandle-Plains Historical Review,* II (1929), 65–97.

Anderson, Latham. "Canby's Service in the New Mexico Campaign." In Robert Underwood Johnson and Clarence Clough Buel, eds., *Battles and Leaders of the Civil War.* New York: The Century Co., 1887–1888, II, 698.

Bell, J. M. "The Campaign of New Mexico, 1862." *War Papers Read Before the Commandry of the State of Wisconsin, Military Order of the Loyal Legion of the United States.* Volume one. Milwaukee: Burdick, Armitage and Allen, 1891.

Bell, James. "The Battle of Val Verde." M. L. Crimmins, editor, *New Mexico Historical Review,* VII (1932), 348–352.

Hall, Martin Hardwick, ed. "An Appraisal of the 1862 New Mexico Campaign: A Confederate Officer's Letter to Natchitoches." *New Mexico Historical Review* 51 (October 1976), 329–333.

Hall, Martin Hardwick, ed. "The Journal of Ebenezer Hanna." *Password* III (January 1958), 14–29.

Hall, Martin Hardwick, ed. "The Taylor Letters: Correspondence from Fort Bliss, 1861." *Military History of Texas and the Southwest* XV, 2 (1979), 53–60.

McLeary, J. H. "History of Green's Brigade." *A Comprehensive History of Texas.* Dudley G. Wooten, ed. Dallas: Scarff, 1898, II, 695–740.

Merchant, S. W. "Fighting with Sibley in New Mexico," *Hunter's Magazine* 1 (November, 1910), 1–20.

"Soldier in the California Column: The Diary of John W. Teal," *Arizona and the West,* XIII, 1 (Spring, 1971), 33–82.

Charles Irion Taylor to Charles S. Taylor in Hall, ed., "The Taylor Letters," 55.

Pettis, George H. "The Confederate Invasion of New Mexico and Arizona," in Robert Underwood Johnson and Clarence Clough Buel, eds., *Battles and Leaders of the Civil War.* New York: The Century Co., 1887–1888), II: 103–111.

Seynn, J. Robert, ed. "A Soldier in New Mexico, 1860–1865." *El Palicio*. LXV (August 1958), 143–145.

Smith, William Henry. "Memoirs of Hank Smith," *Panhandle-Plains Historical Review*, I, 1, (1928), 65–97.

Tate, Michael L., ed. "A Johnny Reb and in Sibley's New Mexico Campaign: Reminiscences of Pvt. Henry C. Wright, 1861–1862." *East Texas Historical Journal*. part one, XXV (1988), 20–33; part two, XXVI (1989), 23–35, 48–60.

Teel, T. T. "Sibley's New Mexico Campaign: Its Object and its Failure," in Robert Underwood Johnson and Clarence Clough Buel, eds., *Battles and Leaders of the Civil War* (New York: The Century Co., 1887–1888), II: 700.

Thompson, Jerry Don., ed., "An Indian Superintendent at the Battle of Valverde: The Civil War Letters of James L. Collins." *Southwestern Historical Quarterly*, CIII, 2, (October, 1999), 215–229.

Thompson, Jerry Don, ed. "'Is This to be the Glory of our Brave Men?' The New Mexico Civil War Journal and Letters of Dr. Henry Jacob 'Hal' Hunter." *New Mexico Historical Review*, (Spring 2001), 535–603.

Thompson, Jerry Don, ed., "With the New Mexico Militia: The Civil War Diary of Major Charles Emil Wesche." *Password*, XXXIX, 1, (1994), 37–47.

Wade, F. S. "Battle of Val Verde." *Confederate Veteran*. XXIX (April 1821), 137–138.

Walker, Henry P., ed. "Soldier in the California Column: The Diary of John W. Teal." *Arizona and the West*. XIII, 1 (spring 1971), 33–82.

Wallace, R. B. "My Experiences in the First Colorado Regiment." *The Colorado Magazine*. (September 1924) The State Historical and Natural History Society of Colorado, Denver, 307–312.

Secondary Sources

Books

Alberts, Don E. *The Battle of Glorieta: Union Victory in the West*. College Station: Texas A&M University Press, 1998.

Edrington, Thomas S., and John Taylor. *The Battle of Glorieta Pass: A Gettysburg in the West, March 26–28, 1862*. Albuquerque: University of New Mexico Press, 1998.

Finch, L. Boyd. *Confederate Pathway to the Pacific: Major Sherod Hunter and Arizona Territory, C.S.A.* Tucson: Arizona Historical Society, 1996.

Frazier, Donald S. *Blood and Treasure: Confederate Empire in the Southwest*. College Station: Texas A&M University Press, 1995.

Ganaway, Loomis Morton. *New Mexico and the Sectional Controversy, 1846–1861*. Santa Fe: The Historical Society of New Mexico, 1944.

Hall, Martin Hardwick. *Sibley's New Mexico Campaign*. Austin: University of Texas Press, 1960; reprint, Albuquerque: University of New Mexico Press, 2000.

Hunt, Aurora. *The Army of the Pacific, 1860–1866*. Glendale: Arthur H. Clark, 1951; reprint, Mechanicsburg, Penn.: Stackpole Books, 2004.

Keleher, William A. *Turmoil in New Mexico, 1846–1868*. Santa Fe: Rydal Press, 1952.

Kerby, Robert Lee. *The Confederate Invasion of New Mexico and Arizona, 1861–1862*. San Jose, Calif.: Westlore, 1958.

Kiser, William S. *Turmoil on the Rio Grande: History of the Mesilla Valley, 1846–1865*. College Station: Texas A&M University Press, 2011.

Masich, Andrew E. *The Civil War in Arizona: The Story of the California Volunteers, 1861–1865*. Norman: University of Oklahoma Press, 2006.

Miller, Darlis A. *The California Column in New Mexico*. Albuquerque: University of New Mexico Press, 1982.

Richards, Leonard L. *The California Gold Rush and the Coming of the Civil War*. New York: Knopf, 2007.

Royce, Josiah. *California, From the Conquest in 1846 to the Second Vigilance Committee in San Francisco: A Study of American Character*. Boston: Houghton Mifflin, 1886.

Taylor, John. *Bloody Valverde: A Civil War Battle on the Rio Grande, February 21, 1862*. Albuquerque: University of New Mexico Press, 1995.

Thompson, Jerry Don. *Henry Hopkins Sibley: Confederate General of the West*. Natchitoches: University of Northwestern Louisiana, 1987.

Thompson, Jerry Don. *John Robert Baylor: Texas Indian Fighter and Confederate Soldier*. Hillsboro, Texas: Hill Junior College Press, 1971.

Articles

Alberts, Don E. "The Battle of Peralta." *New Mexico Historical Review*, LVIII (October 1983), 369–379.

Armstrong, A. F. H. "The Case of Major Isaac Lynde." *New Mexico Historical Review*, XXXVI (January, 1961), 1–35.

Hall, Martin Hardwick. "Colonel Reily's Diplomatic Missions to Chihuahua and Sonora." *New Mexico Historical Review*, XXXI, 3 (July 1956), 232–242.

Finch, L. Boyd. "Sherod Hunter and the Confederates in Arizona." *Journal of Arizona History*. X (fall 1982), 161–173.

Hall, Martin Hardwick. "The Skirmish at Mesilla." *Arizona and the West*, I, 4, (Winter 1959), 343–351.

Silverman, Jason H. "Confederate Ambitions for the Southwest: A New Perspective." *Red River Valley Historical Review*, IV (winter 1979), 62–71.

Thompson, Jerry Don. "Mexican Americans in the Civil War: The Battle of Valverde," Texana, X, 1, (1972), 1–19.

Index

Albuquerque, New Mexico Territory, x, xi, 29, 46, 65, 67, 68, 71, 72, 77, 83, 93, 95, 99, 114
Albuquerque, siege of, 92–95, 97, 109
Alexander, William Lee, 68, 94, 110, 112, 113
Anderson, Allen Latham, 12, 45, 46, 47, 62, 70, 114
Apache Canyon, skirmish at, x, 79–81, 83, 84, 88, 89
Apache Indians, 9, 13, 16, 30, 56, 68, 69, 74, 107
Atrisco, New Mexico Territory, 95

Baylor, George W., 107, 119n11
Baylor, John R., 11, 13, 15, 16, 17, 19–31, 41, 49, 68, 69, 70, 107, 117n8, 119n11, 120n2, 123n9
Bell, Joseph McClellan, 48, 50, 54, 55, 58, 59, 60, 95
Bell, Peter H., 3, 21
Benjamin, Judah P., 28, 29, 69
Bent's Old Fort, 73
Baird, Spruce M., 67, 72
Black Kettle (Cheyenne chief), 74, 79
Bosque Redondo Indian Reservation, 13, 56, 74
Brotherton, David, 54
Buchannan, James, 33

Camp Bisland, Louisiana, battle of, 33
Camp Sibley (San Antonio), 36
Cañada Alamosa, New Mexico Territory, skirmish at, 30
Canby, Edward R. S., ix, x, xi, 7, 8, 9, 13, 14, 23, 24, 27, 29, 40, 41, 43, 44, 46, 47, 53, 54, 58–63, 65, 67, 70, 72, 73, 75, 77, 89, 91–101, 103, 105, 106, 108, 111, 119n22, 120n12, 121n20
Captain Jack (Modoc chief), 7
Carleton, James H., ix, 13, 14, 32, 35, 36, 105, 106, 111, 113, 114
Carnuel Canyon, 94
Carson, Christopher "Kit", x, xi, 13, 40, 53, 54, 56, 58, 72, 91, 119n22
Chapin, Gurden, 6
Chihuahua, Mexican state of, 12, 32, 33, 34, 35, 106
Chivington, John M., 10, 12, 74, 75, 77–81, 83, 84, 87–89, 96, 98, 105, 124n29
Coahuila, Mexican state of, 21, 32
Collins, Thomas Benton, 48

Colorado Territory, 9, 75, 79
Connelly, Henry, 70, 78, 95
Coopwood, Bethel, 20, 21, 29, 30, 93, 100, 101, 108
Cooke, Philip St. George, 10
Crittenden, George Bibb, 5

Davidson, William Lott, 4, 22, 37, 52
Davis Mountains, 38
Davis, Jefferson, ix, 4, 5, 10, 16, 28, 31, 32, 33, 70
Dayton, William Lewis, 4
Department of New Mexico, ix, 7, 13
Department of the Pacific, 14, 35
Dodd, Theodore H., 53, 119n22
Donaldson, James Lowry, 67
Downey, John Gatley, 14

El Paso, Texas, ix, x, 1, 2, 9, 10, 14, 16, 20, 21, 32, 35, 38, 39, 69, 78, 104, 109
Ellis, John William, 59, 61
Enos, Herbert M., 67
Evans, Andrew Wallace, 54
Evans, John, 113
Ewell, Richard Stoddert, 5, 44

Fauntleroy, Thomas Turner, 5
Fillmore, Millard, 4
Floyd, John B., 5
Ford, John S., 17
Fort Bliss, ix, xi, 17, 19, 20, 21, 37–39, 102, 105, 108–111
Fort Breckinridge, 15, 29
Fort Buchanan, 15, 29
Fort Clark, 17, 110, 111
Fort Craig, ix–xi, 9, 15, 26, 29, 30, 39, 40, 43, 44, 46–48, 51, 60, 62, 63, 65, 70, 72, 77, 91, 94, 99–101, 103, 105, 110, 111, 144, 121n20
Fort Davis, 14, 19, 38, 69
Fort Defiance, 7, 8
Fort Fillmore, 4, 9, 14, 15, 20, 22, 28, 29
Fort Garland, 74
Fort Gibson, 16, 17
Fort Lancaster, 111

Fort Leavenworth, 8
Fort Lyon, 56
Fort McLane, 14
Fort Marcy, x, 5
Fort Quitman, 39, 110
Fort Stanton, 15, 24, 26
Fort Stockton, 111
Fort Thorn (or Fort Thorne), 34, 39, 105
Fort Union, x, 9, 29, 46, 65, 67, 68, 72, 73, 75–77, 79, 91, 92, 94, 97, 99, 114, 125n1
Fort Yuma, ix, 14, 35
Frazer, George, 107
Frémont, John C., 56
Fulcrod, Phillip, 100

Galisteo, New Mexico Territory, 72, 83, 95
Garland, Robert R., 24
Gibbs, Alfred, 26, 27
Giesecke, Julius, 38, 48, 49, 68, 83, 84, 88, 89, 101, 102
Gilpin, William C., 9, 11, 12, 74, 78, 113
Glorieta Pass, battle of, x, xi, 10, 33, 36, 49, 74, 75, 78, 80, 82, 84, 87–89, 109, 112
Graydon, James "Paddy," 44, 101, 105, 119n22, 120n5, 120n12
Grayson, John Breckenridge, 5
Greeley, Horace, 5, 74
Green, Tom, x, xi, 10, 34, 36, 38, 41–43, 51, 53–55, 58, 59, 61, 63, 71, 72, 83, 88, 92, 93, 95–97, 100–102, 104, 121n21
Guaymas, Mexico, 32, 35
Gwyther, George, 14

Hall, Robert Henry, 47, 54, 55, 58, 119n22, 120n12, 121n20
Halleck, Henry W., 6, 92
Hardeman, Peter, 25
Hardeman, William P. "Old Gotch," 93, 94, 119n11
Hays, John C., 42, 49
Helm, Thomas, 68
Herbert, P. T., 119n11
Henderson, J. Pinckney, 2
Hollister, Ovando J., 8, 9, 11–12, 30, 37, 40, 43, 44, 59, 60, 62, 72, 73, 75–77, 79, 80, 81, 83–87, 89, 92, 94–101, 103, 106, 111, 113, 121n21, 125n47, 125n1

Houston, Sam, 4, 33, 42
Hunter, Sherrod, ix, 106–107

Ickis, Alonzo Ferdinand, 7, 8

Johnson's Ranch, (Cañoncito) skirmish at, 78, 79, 81
Jones, John Marshall, 24
Journedad del Muerto, 27
Juárez, Benito, 32–33

Kearney, Stephen Watts, 56
Kelley, Robert P., 70
Knights of the Golden Circle, 57
Kozlowski's Ranch, 77, 79, 87, 124n29

La Joya, New Mexico Territory, 99
Lancers, 37, 53, 54
Lane, James Henry, 12
Lane, William Carr, 1
Lang, Willis, 53, 54, 121n23
Lewis, William Henry, 77
Limitar, New Mexico Territory, 103
Lockridge, Samuel A. (a.k.a. William Kissane), 40, 41, 55, 57–58, 61, 112, 122n31
Longstreet, James, 5
Lord, Richard S. C., 59
Loring, William H., 5, 8
Los Lunas, New Mexico Territory, 95
Lynde, Isaac, 9, 14–16, 22–29, 117n11, 117n22

McCall, George Archibald, 1
McCarthy, James, 69
McCown, Jerome B., 112
McKee, James Cooper, 15, 21, 23–28, 117n8, 117n14, 117n18, 117n20
McLeary, James Harvey, 37, 38, 43, 50, 51, 58, 60, 68, 93, 94
McNally, Christopher Hely, 23
McNeill, Henry C., 100
McRae, Alexander, 47, 48, 50, 53, 54, 57–59, 61, 95
McWilley, M. H., 4

Magdalena Mountains (Sierra Magdalena), 101–102
Magdalena, New Mexico, 102
Maxey, Samuel Bell, 104
"Mays Massacre," 69
Mays, Reuben E., 69
Merrick, Morgan Wolfe, 19, 20, 22, 28–30, 69, 117n8, 117n14
Mesa de la Contedera (Black Mesa), 48, 54
Mesilla, New Mexico Territory, ix–xi, 4, 6, 14, 16, 20, 22–26, 28, 29, 70, 99, 101, 104, 107, 111, 114
Mesilla, skirmish at, 22–23
Mexico, Republic of, 1, 2, 32–35
Military units, Confederate
  Army of New Mexico, x, xi, 4, 31, 39, 63, 67, 89, 97, 105, 108–109, 111–112, 114
  Fifth Texas Mounted Rifles, 4, 6, 33, 37–38, 42, 48, 57, 61, 78, 80, 95, 100
  First Texas Mounted Rifles, 34, 106, 119n11
  Fourth Texas Mounted Rifles, xi, 33, 36, 38, 49, 50, 63, 82
  P. T. Herbert's Texas cavalry battalion, 119n11
  San Elizario Spies and Guides, 21, 23, 29
  Second Texas Mounted Rifles, ix, 16,–17, 30, 49, 72, 79, 92
  Seventh Texas Mounted Rifles, ix, 51, 104
  Sibley's Texas Brigade (*see* Army of New Mexico)
  Teel's Battery, 43, 51–53, 58, 92, 120n2
  Third Texas Mounted Rifles, 94, 105
  Valverde Battery, 102
Military units, Union
  "California Column," ix, 13, 14, 105, 106, 114
  Dodd's independent company of Colorado volunteers, 53, 119n22
  Eighth California Infantry, 12
  Fifth New Mexico Infantry, 48, 119n22, 120n12
  Fifth U.S. Infantry, 12, 15, 47, 54, 59, 61, 77, 111
  First California Cavalry, 13, 14
  First Colorado Volunteers, x, 8, 11, 12, 67, 72, 74, 75, 78, 84, 98, 113, 114
  First New Mexico Infantry, xi, 53, 56, 91, 120n12
  First U.S. Dragoons, 13, 44
  Fourth New Mexico Infantry, 76, 120n12
  Fourth U.S. Cavalry, 13
  Graydon's Spy Company, 44, 119n22, 120n12
  Hall's battery, 47, 54, 55, 58, 119n22, 120n12), 121n20

McRae's battery, 48, 50, 54, 57–59, 61, 95, 119n22, 120n12, 121n20
Mounted Rifles Regiment, 5, 48, 56, 57
Second California Cavalry, 106
Second Colorado Volunteers ("Pike's Peakers"), 53, 54, 56, 72, 79,83, 84
Second New Mexico Infantry, 62, 120n12
Seventh U.S. Infantry, ix, 15, 16, 27, 76
Tenth U.S. Infantry, 7, 40, 119n22
Third Colorado Cavalry, 78
Third U.S. Cavalry, ix, 54, 57, 119n22
Third U.S. Dragoons, 48
Minks, John H., 30
Monterrey, battle of, 37, 42, 49, 104
Morris, Robert M., 30
Mountain Meadows Massacre, 13
Munroe, John, 4

Navajo Indians, 9, 10, 13, 56, 68, 74
Need, William, 5
New Mexico Territory, ix, 2, 3, 10, 13–15, 17, 22, 31, 34, 68, 100
Nicholas (Mescalero chief), 69
Noel, Theophilus, 71, 108
Northern District of New Mexico, 76, 92
Nuevo Léon, Mexican state of, 32

Ojo del Pueblo, New Mexico Territory, 102, 105
Oldham, Williamson Simpson, 113
Organ Mountains, 24
Oury, Granville H., 6

Paradito, New Mexico Territory, skirmish at, 40
Paul, Gabriel R., 76, 91, 92, 94, 105.
Peralta, New Mexico Territory, xi, 95–98, 100, 109, 110
Peralta, battle of, xi, 95–98, 100, 109, 110
Pesqueira, Ignacio, 34, 35
Peticolas, A. B., 21, 50–53, 55, 59, 60, 62, 68, 70–72, 81–83, 86–89, 91, 93, 94, 96, 97, 99–103, 105, 108–110
Pettis, George, 30, 44, 50, 58, 60, 61, 87, 98, 105
Phillips, Joseph, 119n11
Picacho Pass, Arizona Territory, skirmish at, ix, 106, 107

Pierce, Franklin, 5
Pigeon's Ranch, skirmish at, x, 74, 77, 79, 81, 83, 84, 87, 124n29
Pima Indians, 106
Pinos Altos mines, 68
Piño, Miguel Estanislado, x, 40, 62
Polk, James K., 2, 56
Pyron, Charles Lynn, x, 30, 49–50, 67, 72, 79–81, 83, 84, 95

Raguet, Charles Mansfield, 110
Raguet, Henry W., 49, 50, 54, 58, 88, 112
Randolph, George Wythe, 70
Reily, James (Colonel), 32–36, 49, 93, 106
Reynolds, Alexander Welch, 5
Rhett, Thomas Grimke, 5
Roberts, Benjamin S., 5, 15, 46–48, 53, 61, 62
Royce, Josiah, 13
Rusk, Thomas Jefferson, 33, 82

Sabinal, New Mexico Territory, 99
San Agustín Springs, 24, 25
San Agustín Springs, skirmish at, 25–26
San Mateo Mountains, xi, 101–103
Sand Creek Massacre, 74, 79
Sandina Mountains, 92
Santa Fe, New Mexico Territory, x, xi, 1–3, 5, 6, 8, 10, 24, 27, 29, 44, 56, 65, 67, 70, 72, 73, 75, 77–79, 87–89, 91–94, 114, 117n3
Santa Fe Trail, x, 14, 83. 86, 87
Sayers, Joseph Draper, 61
Selden, Henry Raymond, 46, 59
Scott, Winfield, 4, 7, 10, 92, 104
Scurry, William R., x, 33, 36, 49, 50, 51, 53, 59, 65, 72, 82–89, 91, 92, 95, 96, 100–102, 106, 108
Shannon, Denman William, 65, 85
Shropshire, John S., 78–80, 85, 88, 112
Sibley, Henry Hopkins, ix–xi, 5, 7, 9, 10, 13, 31, 32, 34–36, 38–44, 46, 49, 51, 57, 60, 63, 65, 67, 68–72, 74, 75, 77, 78, 83, 91–96, 98–101, 104, 105, 108–110, 114
Slough, John P., x, xi, 10, 12, 73–78, 83–85, 87–89, 92, 125n47
Smith, Edmund Kirby, 7

Smith, William Henry "Hank," 6, 25, 39, 71, 72, 91
Socorro, New Mexico Territory, 70, 71
Sonora, Mexican state of, 12, 32, 33, 34, 35, 106
Starr, James Franklin, xi, 36, 43, 48, 51, 55, 60, 67, 77, 93, 94, 100, 108–113
Steele, William, 72, 82, 94, 95, 104–105, 111, 119n11
Steen, Alexander Early, 5
Sumner, Edwin V., 14
Sutton, John Schuyler, 61, 112

Tappan, Samuel F., 12, 73–74, 98
Taylor, Milam, 19, 21–23, 25, 27, 39
Taylor, Richard, 7, 10, 42
Taylor, Zachary, 13, 42, 104
Teal, John W., 106
Teel, Trevanian T., 5, 43, 51–53, 58, 92, 96
Terrazas, Luis, 34, 35
Texan Santa Fe Expedition, 2
Thomas, Lorenzo, 62

Valverde, battle of, x, xi, 7, 10, 33, 41, 42, 46–49, 56, 57, 59–62, 65, 70, 72, 88, 98, 109, 114, 121n20, 121n21
Van Dorn, Earl, 9, 49
Van Horn, Texas, 20
Vidaurri, Santiago, 32

Wade, F. S., 49, 53–55
Walker, William, 40, 57
Waller, Edwin, 25
Wingate, Benjamin, 54, 59
Worth, William Jennings, 36–37
Wright, George, 14, 35
Wright, Henry C., 55, 56, 58, 60, 61, 63, 71

CPSIA information can be obtained at www.ICGtesting.com
Printed in the USA
LVOW07s0607111115

461925LV00003B/6/P

9 781933 337654